FINANCE FOR THE GENERAL MANAGER

A DAY WITH A CEO

BRIAN MOORE & MICHELLE JEFFREY

Copyright © 2012 by Brian Moore
All rights reserved.
ISBN: 0615664911
ISBN-13: 978-0615664910

WHY THIS BOOK?

This book was created as a result of several decades of General Management experience covering many companies in different industries predominantly in the USA, Europe and Asia. The companies have been of varying size ranging from small family businesses to publicly traded companies. Most of this experience was gained as a group CEO directly leading a central team and overseeing the Profit and Loss performance of many subsidiary company teams running stand-alone businesses.

The paradox is that as my career progressed, life became more complicated and the data bank of experience increased, but the basic requirements of the General Management (GM) role appeared to be much simpler. The need to keep focused on basic questions and the need to keep asking "*WHY ARE YOU DOING THAT?*" became more relevant. *A key task of the top Executives in any organization is to simplify complex subjects for the team to understand and run with.*

This is the **second book** in the *A Day With a CEO* series. It focuses on **FINANCE,** which is the most important area that any GM requires to understand because a ***BUSINESS HAS THE MAIN OBJECTIVE OF MAKING MONEY.*** So, how that money is created and recorded in a set of accounts is fundamentally important.

The book includes detailed exercises that have been simplified to ease the understanding of the financial concepts and includes exercises and schematics that I have used in my career, before qualifying as an accountant, to help understand business finance. It is a collaborative effort with Michelle who started her career as a professional accountant and has brought some of the more traditional accounting treatments into the book.

Although targeted at General Managers, the content will be of use to anyone interested in how a business should be managed, especially early career managers with aspirations to become a GM. It will also be of use to provide financial advice to the *non-financial manager.*

Enjoy the book and remember two things — ***CASH is KING*** and keep asking ***WHY?***

*This is the book that I wish that I had at the start of my career to act as a **Financial Guide**. I would certainly still be carrying it with me.*

AREAS OF FINANCIAL ACTIVITY

In any business there are three major areas of financial activity. For the very large companies each area would have dedicated and specialist staff involved. For the very small businesses they would probably be handled by one accountant / owner manager. Regardless of size, it is important to understand what they are and how they interrelate with each other.

CORPORATE FINANCE

This area looks after the creation and management of the finance **(CASH)** required to start and support the business. It would typically involve the following activities: raising money, banking arrangements, treasury management (managing the cash balances), foreign exchange, and equity / share structure / distributions.

PROFIT AND LOSS REPORTING

This is the ongoing reporting of the business through the three main accounts — PROFIT & LOSS, CASH FLOW AND BALANCE SHEET. These accounts are important as they represent the performance measurement of the business and are used for many purposes — raising cash, supporting loan arrangements, external valuations and of course, the performance of the management team led by the General Manager / CEO. In other words, this is your bottom line scorecard.

COSTING SYSTEMS

Most companies have a costing system to provide a more detailed tool for controlling the transactional activity of the products within the business. There are many different costing systems, but they virtually all use some form of ABSORPTION COSTING principles.

The focus of this book is on the last two areas as this is where CEOs / General Managers will have to focus most of their time in order to manage the business effectively and to ensure that it is reported correctly. The book also explains the interactions between the costing systems and the Profit and Loss accounting.

INDEX

Power	4
Introduction	5
Business Definitions Objectives	6
Main Role of the Finance Team	7
Financial Schematic / Rules of Finance	8-9
Main Accounts — Profit & Loss / Cash Flow / Balance Sheet	10
Finance Awareness Exercise / Starting a Business	11-20
Power of 1% / Savings Analysis	21-22
Profit = Cash?	23
Break-Even Charts	24
Profit	25
Absorption Costing	26-54
Cash	55
Financial Planning and Budget	56-57
Savings — Real or Not?	58
Dealing With the Sales Team. Review Sales Forecast	59-63
Measurement	64
KPI	65
Numbers That You Should Know	66
Information That You Should Know	67
Questions That You Should Ask	68-69
Time / Accuracy / Cost	70
Activities That Can Cost A Lot	71-79
Business Review Process	80-81
Fraud	82-83
Dealing With Accountants	84
Basic Tips for a Good Financial Performance	85
Basic Accounting Entries	86-87
Valuing a Business	88
Analytical Techniques / Financial Tools	89-91
Ratio Analysis	92
Accounting Standards	93
Dealing With Private Equity / Venture Capitalists	94
Psychological Points to Ponder	95

APPENDICES

CHECK LISTS	A2-A5
COMMON TERMS AND ABBREVIATIONS	A6-A10

POWER

SIMPLE CONCEPT

> There are many types of power, but in the context of a CEO / GM the largest power base is PERFORMANCE, or more specifically **FINANCIAL PERFORMANCE.**
> As a general rule the better your results are, then the more power and freedom that you will have to get on and do the job your way!
> The poorer the results, the more those that judge and control you will want to become involved in your business.

BAD RESULTS WILL ULTIMATELY GET YOU FIRED

INTRODUCTION

This book is intended for General Managers (GMs) to explain the basics of finance! How to make money and how to improve profitability.

The experience of the authors is considered to be particularly relevant. Brian started his working life as an apprentice on the shop floor and worked his way up through line management to become a GM and having to understand finance along the way through hands-on experience. He then obtained a formal finance qualification (ACMA). Michelle had a more traditional accounting background having earned an accounting degree at college, then joining one of the main accounting firms for training. Her working experience started in internal audit / special investigations and progressed with public company and SOX experience to become a senior finance executive in a manufacturing company. When Michelle and Brian started working together, they realized having worked from two different perspectives that there was a need for a book that GMs could easily understand in order to become a more effective executive. This book is the result of that collaboration. The blend of general management and specialist financial training has hopefully resulted in a useful and easy-to-read book.

The simplicity of the book is deliberate. If you understand these basic numbers and reports and how they all interrelate, the only thing you have to do in the more complex financial reports is to determine where they fit into the BASIC reporting structure and relate back to basics. The focus throughout the book is the need for a business to "Make Money," real CASH.

NO CASH = NO BUSINESS

In the book are several analytical exercises coupled with a questioning approach from the GM's perspective.

Absorption costing forms a major part of the book because it is relevant to so many businesses ranging from the High Street fast food outlet through to the largest multinationals. The lack of understanding of absorption costing opportunities and potential problems is widespread amongst managers and by quite a few accountants who have not had the hands-on operating experience to understand some of its complexities.

BUSINESS DEFINITIONS

ORGANIZATION
A collection of people and assets that pursue a common purpose

BUSINESS
An organization that has the principle objective of making a **PROFIT**

STOP AND THINK! THEN REFLECT.

> *IF YOU WORK IN A BUSINESS, THEN YOU ARE PAID BY THAT BUSINESS TO HELP IT MAKE MONEY. ALL OF THE MANY THINGS THAT CONSUME YOUR DAY AND THE MANY IDEALS AND INITIATIVES THAT YOU ARE CONDITIONED WITH ARE ALL A MEANS TO ACHIEVE THAT MAIN OBJECTIVE OF MAKING MONEY. I HAVE ARGUED THIS MANY TIMES AND HEARD MANY OTHER REASONS WHY PEOPLE THINK A BUSINESS EXISTS. BUT THE FAILURE MODE MAKES THIS POINT COMPELLINGLY OBVIOUS.*

NO CASH = NO BUSINESS

WHAT VALUE ARE CUSTOMER RELATIONS IF YOU ARE NOT THERE TO SERVE THEM?

MAIN ROLE OF THE FINANCE TEAM

To keep a numerate record of business activity (score keepers).

To provide a set of accounts for the authorities to check.
Mainly for taxation purposes.

To provide forecasting guidance and direction from a numerate perspective.

To evaluate the financial impact of business decisions.

To ensure that the business is financially prudent and fiscally responsible.

To manage and support the audit of the business.

To provide financial / analytical support to the company strategy.

To ensure that all financial reporting is accurate and consistent.

Remember that the Finance function does not run the business. It can sometimes seem that way because they have access to information, which is a KEY power base.

By all means, form a close working relationship with the Finance team, but always stay focused as a General Manager as YOU will be responsible for
DELIVERING THE PROFIT.

BASIC FINANCIAL SCHEMATIC

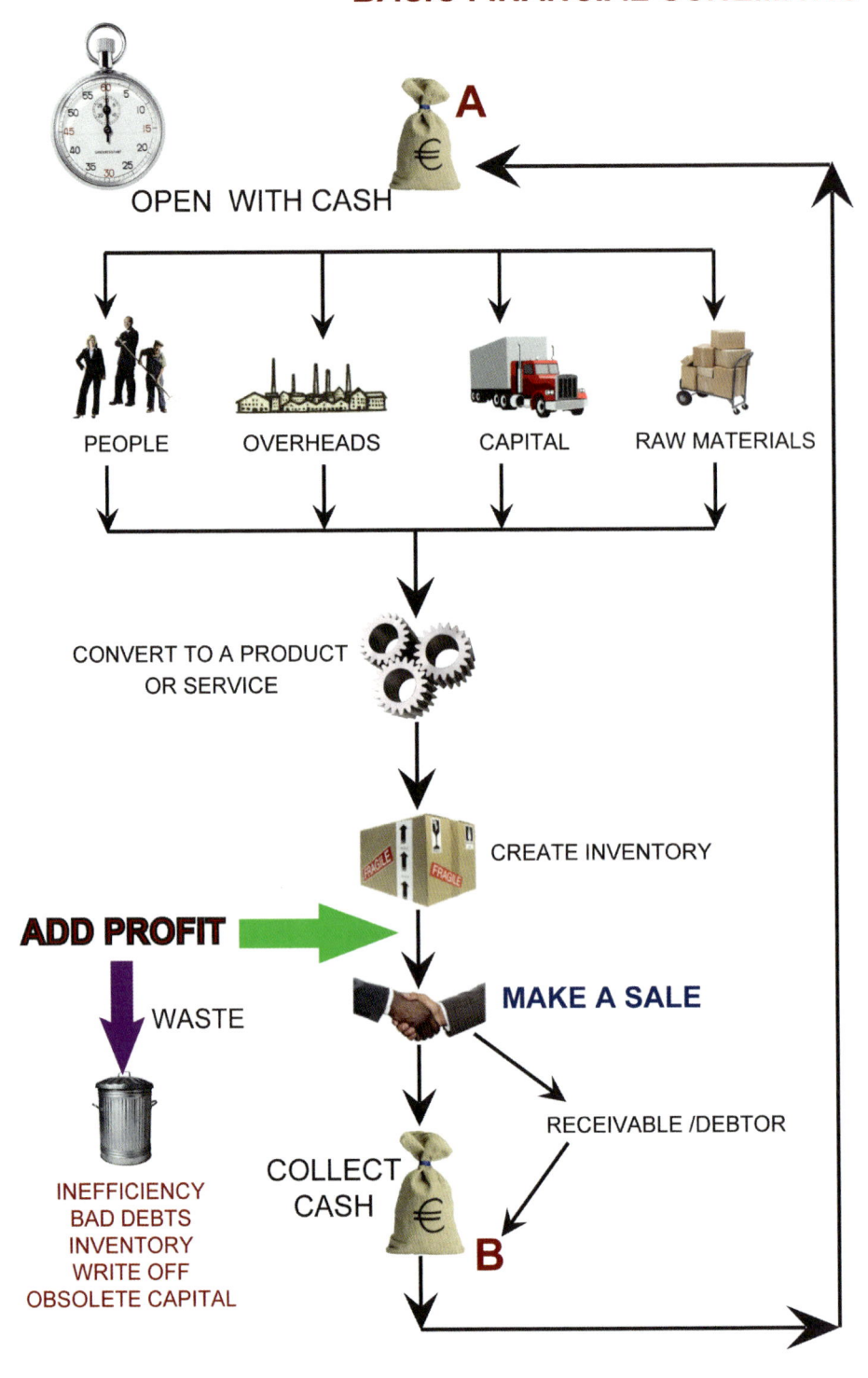

A — OPEN WITH CASH

- PEOPLE
- OVERHEADS
- CAPITAL
- RAW MATERIALS

CONVERT TO A PRODUCT OR SERVICE

CREATE INVENTORY

ADD PROFIT

WASTE
- INEFFICIENCY
- BAD DEBTS
- INVENTORY WRITE OFF
- OBSOLETE CAPITAL

MAKE A SALE

RECEIVABLE / DEBTOR

COLLECT CASH — **B**

PAGE 8 — COPYRIGHT BRIAN MOORE — A DAY WITH A CEO — FINANCE

RULES OF FINANCE
Related to Schematic

DO NOT RUN OUT OF CASH

GO FROM A TO B AS FAST AS POSSIBLE

ADD AS MUCH PROFIT AS MARKET WILL STAND

OPERATE AS EFFICIENTLY AS POSSIBLE

REDUCE WASTE

DO NOT TIE CASH UP IN LARGE ASSETS / INVENTORY

MAXIMIZE CREDITORS (Source of finance, but do not over do it!)

MINIMIZE DEBTORS (Collect CASH quickly)

EVERY THING YOU DO WILL IMPACT THIS SCHEMATIC

Consider all your actions and plans and make sure that they are directed to the efficient operation of this schematic. If you are unable to see how, have another look. You may have missed something.
If you are still unable to see how your action is improving this schematic,

WHY ARE YOU DOING IT ?

FINANCE BASIC REPORTS

PROFIT & LOSS ACCOUNT

A report covering a period of time that includes all the revenues, incomes and cost expenditures. Plus any valuation changes to the assets related to that time period. The difference between the income and the costs being the PROFIT, which will be charged to the BALANCE SHEET as an asset.

CASH FLOW REPORT

A report covering a period of time that only shows the movements of CASH in and out of the business with the opening and starting point being the CASH IN HAND. This is the most important report to determine business viability and capability to trade.

The relationship between P&L account requires to be understood as it is more than possible for a business to be showing a healthy profit but FAIL because it runs out of CASH!

NO CASH = NO BUSINESS

BALANCE SHEET

A snapshot of all the ASSETS and LIABILITIES of a business at any moment in time. Usually at the start and end of the periods that the P&L and CASH FLOW accounts are related to. It lists all the assets and liabilities of the business and reconciles them so that they BALANCE.

FINANCIAL AWARENESS EXERCISE
Pages 12 to 20

OBJECTIVE

This exercise is intended to illustrate the relationship between Profit and Cash as a result of various actions that can be taken within a business to improve profitability.

It uses very simple accounts PROFIT & LOSS, CASH FLOW and BALANCE SHEET to illustrate the impact and interactivity of the accounting treatments. Inflation has been ignored to ensure that the accounting entries can be more easily understood.

Above all, it is intended to provide an awareness of the importance of certain basic management actions on the profitability of a business without getting too confused with the accounting treatments.

APPROACH

The exercise shows how a business starts and the opening balance sheet.

One year's trading is then carried out and the various accounting entries in the main accounts are shown.

A budget is prepared for the second year, which is rejected by the GM as unacceptable.

The GM calls for some profit improvement ideas for the BUDGET and these are then evaluated from a financial and business perspective.

The proposed sales forecast is also critically evaluated in the section about Sales Finances on page 60 — 61.

If you would like to understand more about the basic accounting entries and the wonders of DOUBLE ENTRY, DEBITs, CREDITs and T accounts, they have been included at the back of this book on pages 86 — 87.

STARTING A BUSINESS

THREE ESSENTIALS TO START A BUSINESS

AN IDEA HOW TO MAKE MONEY

CASH

A PLAN

RAISING THE INITIAL CASH IS A KEY REQUIREMENT.

THIS MAY INVOLVE LENGTHY DISCUSSIONS WITH
THE PROVIDERS OF CAPITAL (CASH).

A BUSINESS PLAN WITH NUMBERS IN WILL BE ESSENTIAL.

ESSENTIALS TO KEEP A BUSINESS

DO NOT RUN OUT OF CASH

MAKE MONEY

THE PLAN WORKS

EXECUTION EFFECTIVE

BASIC ASSUMPTIONS CORRECT

MAINTAIN SUPPORT OF FINANCIERS

GOOD LUCK

PLUS OF COURSE

KEEP FOCUSED ON THE FINANCIAL PERFORMANCE

OPENING ACCOUNTS FOR A NEW BUSINESS

DAY 1

The company has raised CASH from 2 sources:

A bank loan of 30000 of which interest is due at 10% pa.

Personal CASH from the owner, 40000 which is the equity / shares

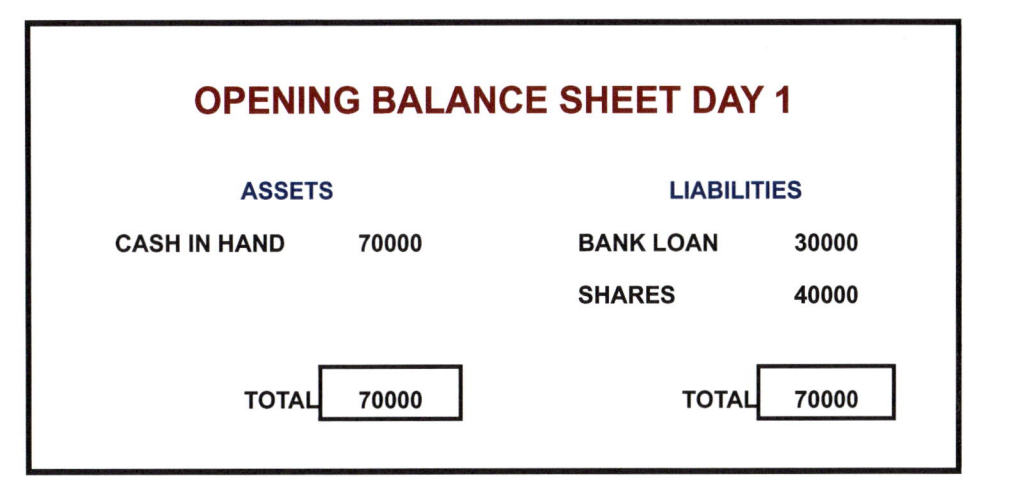

OPENING BALANCE SHEET DAY 1

ASSETS		LIABILITIES	
CASH IN HAND	70000	BANK LOAN	30000
		SHARES	40000
TOTAL	**70000**	**TOTAL**	**70000**

The BALANCE SHEET is a snapshot of the business at a SPECIFIC TIME.

The balance sheet shows how much CASH there is and where it comes from.

At this simple level, the BALANCE aspect of a balance sheet is clear.

BUSINESS COMMENCES.

Reporting is through two main accounts.

Profit & Loss
CASH Flow

These accounts record activity over a time period.

At the end of that TIME period,

A CLOSING BALANCE SHEET IS CREATED

Pages 14 and 15 illustrate with an example how these accounts are prepared.

FINANCIAL REPORT FOR YEAR JUST ENDED

YEAR 1 of a NEW BUSINESS

ACCOUNTING ENTRIES

#	BUSINESS TRANSACTIONS	P&L	CASH	BS	NOTE
1	OPEN CASH 70K		70000	70000	SEE PAGE 13
2	PAY BANK INTEREST 3K PA	-3000	-3000		2
3	PAY RENT 20K PER ANNUM	-20000	-20000		1
4	SALES 50K / MONTH 600000 TOTAL	600000			3
5	SALES ON ONE MONTH CREDIT 550K COLLECTED		550000		4
6	SALES RECEIVABLE DUE 1 MONTH 50K AT YEAR END			50000	16
7	ADMIN PAYROLL EXPENSED IN YEAR AND PAID CASH 30K	-30000	-30000		5
8	DIRECT PAYROLL PAID CASH IN YEAR 90K	-90000	-90000		26
9	SUNDRY EXPENSES PAID CASH IN YEAR 25K	-25000	-25000		6
10	DIRECT MATERIALS USED IN PRODUCTION 200K	-200000		-200000	15
11	PRODUCTION SCRAPPED 5K MATERIAL	-5000		-5000	11
12	DIRECT OVERHEADS ALL CASH PAID IN YEAR 120K	-120000	-120000		14
13	DIRECT MATERIALS PURCHASED WERE 300K			300000	17
14	DIRECT MATERIALS ON 30 DAYS CREDIT 275K PAID IN YEAR		-275000		9
15	DIRECT MATERIAL CREDITOR 1 MONTH 25K			-25000	10
16	A CUSTOMER NOT PAYING 15K PROVISION CREATED	-15000		-15000	18
17	YEAR END INVENTORY WROTE OFF 20K OBSOLETE MATERIAL	-20000		-20000	7
18	YEAR END INVENTORY CHECK REVEALED 30K MAY NOT SELL PROVISION CREATED	-30000		-30000	8

BUSINESS PERFORMANCE

	P&L	CASH	BS	NOTE
PROFIT CREATED	42000	→	42000	A
CASH CONSUMED		-13000		NOTE!!!
CASH BALANCE YEAR END		57000	57000	C

NOTE THE PROFIT AND CLOSING CASH MOVED TO THE BALANCE SHEET

INVENTORY CALCULATION ON BALANCE SHEET

DELIVERED	300000	NOTE 17
USED IN PRODUCTION	-200000	NOTE 15
SCRAPPED	-5000	NOTE 11
WRITTEN OFF	-20000	NOTE 7
PROVISION DOUBTFUL SALE	-30000	NOTE 8
	45000	NOTE 25

THREE MAIN ACCOUNTS FOR YEAR 1 PERFORMANCE

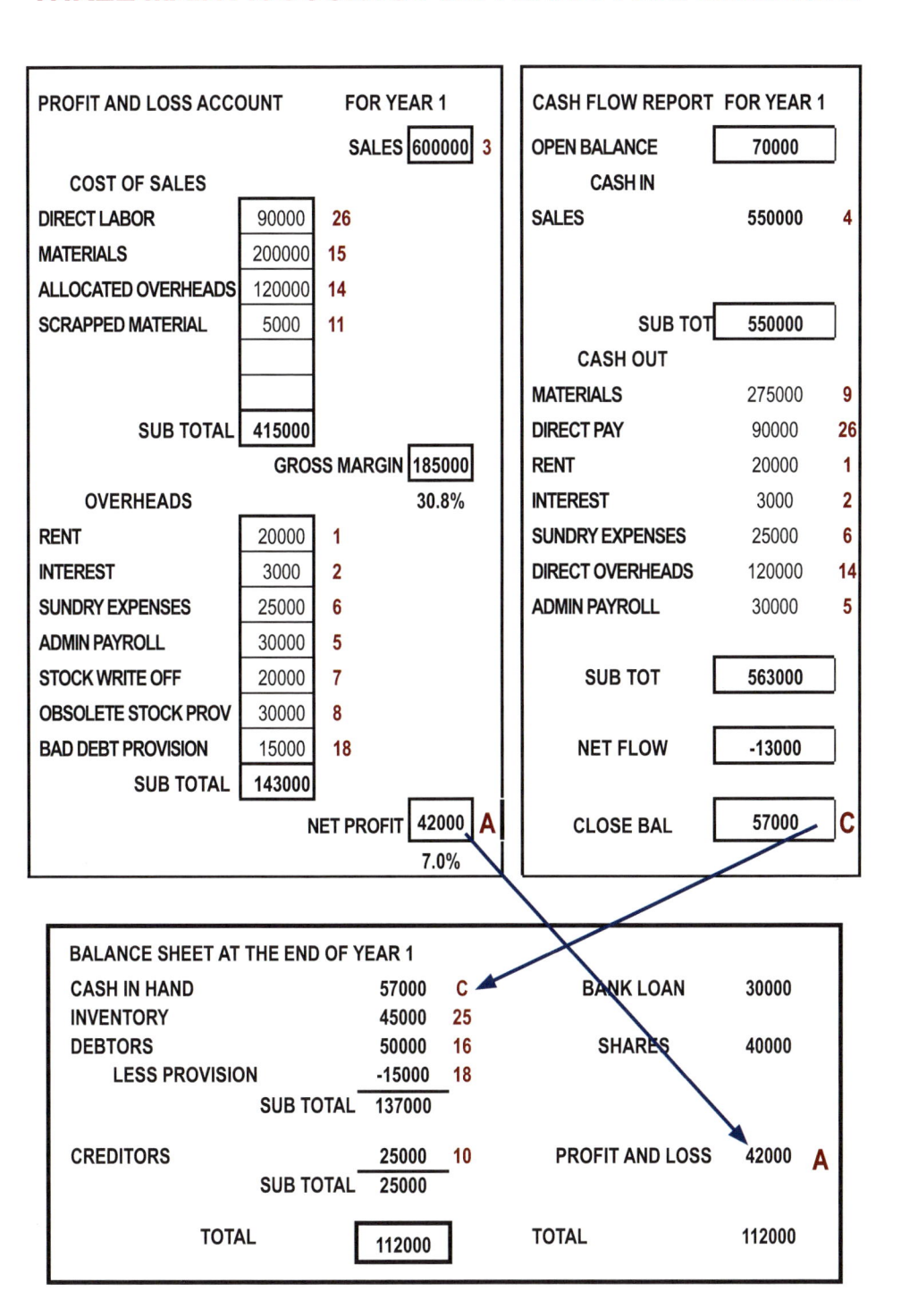

PROFIT AND LOSS ACCOUNT — FOR YEAR 1

SALES **600000** 3

COST OF SALES

DIRECT LABOR	90000	26
MATERIALS	200000	15
ALLOCATED OVERHEADS	120000	14
SCRAPPED MATERIAL	5000	11
SUB TOTAL	415000	

GROSS MARGIN **185000**
30.8%

OVERHEADS

RENT	20000	1
INTEREST	3000	2
SUNDRY EXPENSES	25000	6
ADMIN PAYROLL	30000	5
STOCK WRITE OFF	20000	7
OBSOLETE STOCK PROV	30000	8
BAD DEBT PROVISION	15000	18
SUB TOTAL	143000	

NET PROFIT **42000** A
7.0%

CASH FLOW REPORT FOR YEAR 1

OPEN BALANCE **70000**

CASH IN

SALES 550000 4

SUB TOT **550000**

CASH OUT

MATERIALS	275000	9
DIRECT PAY	90000	26
RENT	20000	1
INTEREST	3000	2
SUNDRY EXPENSES	25000	6
DIRECT OVERHEADS	120000	14
ADMIN PAYROLL	30000	5

SUB TOT **563000**

NET FLOW **-13000**

CLOSE BAL **57000** C

BALANCE SHEET AT THE END OF YEAR 1

CASH IN HAND		57000	C	BANK LOAN	30000
INVENTORY		45000	25		
DEBTORS		50000	16	SHARES	40000
LESS PROVISION		-15000	18		
	SUB TOTAL	137000			
CREDITORS		25000	10	PROFIT AND LOSS	42000 A
	SUB TOTAL	25000			
TOTAL		**112000**		TOTAL	112000

A DAY WITH A CEO — FINANCE   COPYRIGHT BRIAN MOORE   PAGE 15

A BUDGET HAS BEEN PREPARED FOR YR 2
YEAR 2 BUDGET

The team have built the following assumptions into the BUDGET on the opposite page.

1 Profit and Loss account is the SAME as trading and all costs are the same, including the same amount of scrap and provisions, etc.

2 This will result in the following changes to the cash flow and the balance sheet.

CASH FLOW

Sales income now full year as credit 1 month negated at 600000	Note 20
Material spend also for the full year at 300000	Note 22
All other cash flows remain the same. NET IN FLOW 12000	Note 21

BALANCE SHEET

The Profit & Loss balance is doubled to 84K (2 Years Profit at 42K).

INVENTORY CALCULATION IS

OPEN	45000
DELIVERED	300000
USED IN PRODUCTION	-200000
SCRAPPED	-5000
WRITTEN OFF	-20000
PROVISION DOUBTFUL SALE	-30000
	90000 NOTE 14

PROFIT V. CASH RECONCILIATION

PROFIT 42000 CASH 12000. DIFFERENCE   **30000**

RECONCILIATION

INVENTORY PURCHASED ABOVE REQUIRED	100000
STOCK WRITE OFFS (3)	-55000
INCREASED CREDITOR PROVISION	-15000
	30000

DO YOU THINK THIS IS A GOOD USE OF CASH?
FUND INVENTORY AND PROVISIONS?

GENERAL MANAGERS RESPONSE TO BUDGET PROPOSAL
REJECT AND CALL FOR PROFIT IMPROVEMENT IDEAS

SEE PAGES 18, 19 AND 20 FOR EVALUATION OF SOME IDEAS.

THREE MAIN ACCOUNTS FOR THE YEAR 2 BUDGET

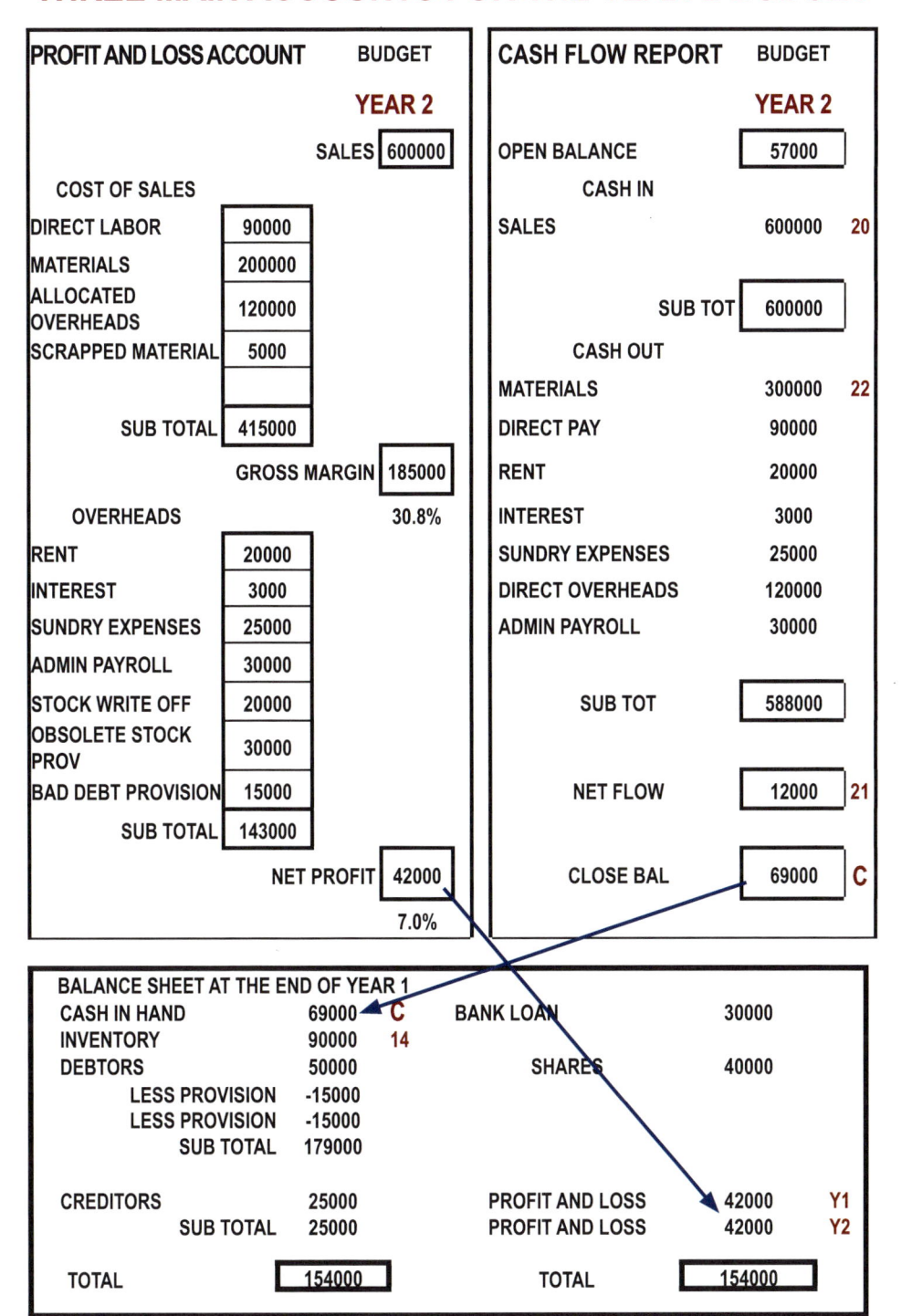

PROFIT AND LOSS ACCOUNT — BUDGET YEAR 2

		SALES 600000
COST OF SALES		
DIRECT LABOR	90000	
MATERIALS	200000	
ALLOCATED OVERHEADS	120000	
SCRAPPED MATERIAL	5000	
SUB TOTAL	415000	
	GROSS MARGIN	185000
		30.8%
OVERHEADS		
RENT	20000	
INTEREST	3000	
SUNDRY EXPENSES	25000	
ADMIN PAYROLL	30000	
STOCK WRITE OFF	20000	
OBSOLETE STOCK PROV	30000	
BAD DEBT PROVISION	15000	
SUB TOTAL	143000	
	NET PROFIT	42000
		7.0%

CASH FLOW REPORT — BUDGET YEAR 2

OPEN BALANCE	57000	
CASH IN		
SALES	600000	20
SUB TOT	600000	
CASH OUT		
MATERIALS	300000	22
DIRECT PAY	90000	
RENT	20000	
INTEREST	3000	
SUNDRY EXPENSES	25000	
DIRECT OVERHEADS	120000	
ADMIN PAYROLL	30000	
SUB TOT	588000	
NET FLOW	12000	21
CLOSE BAL	69000	C

BALANCE SHEET AT THE END OF YEAR 1

CASH IN HAND	69000	C	BANK LOAN	30000
INVENTORY	90000	14		
DEBTORS	50000		SHARES	40000
LESS PROVISION	-15000			
LESS PROVISION	-15000			
SUB TOTAL	179000			
CREDITORS	25000		PROFIT AND LOSS	42000	Y1
SUB TOTAL	25000		PROFIT AND LOSS	42000	Y2
TOTAL	154000		TOTAL	154000

A DAY WITH A CEO — FINANCE   COPYRIGHT BRIAN MOORE

PROFIT IMPROVEMENT IDEAS...
WITH A FINANCIAL EVALUATION

The impact on PROFIT and CASH has been calculated using the P&L on Page 17

Sales director proposes increasing the prices by 1%. Expects to lose 2% sales as a result.	SALES	PROFIT	CASH
Sales increase is 1% ALL PRICE	6000		
Profit and CASH increases in line with sales 100%		6000	6000
Sales lost at 2%	-12000		
At this level would presume that all costs are the same except the direct material + labor			
Direct cost is 48% (90K+200K / 600K) lost contribution 52% on 12000 sales		-6240	
Lose cash on 12000 sales, but not spend 48% on material			-6240
NET POSITION REDUCE PROFIT BY	-6000	-240	-240

Finance director wants a 5% sales increase, but the sales director thinks they would lose 5% of sales.	SALES	PROFIT	CASH
Sales increase is 5% ALL PRICE	30000		
Profit and CASH increases in line with sales 100%		30000	30000
Sales lost at 5%	-30000		
At this level would presume that all costs remain the same except the direct material + labor			
Direct cost content is 48% (90K+200K / 600K) lost contribution 52% on 30000 sales		-15600	
Lose cash on 30000 sales, but not spend 48% on material			-15600
NET POSITION INCREASE PROFIT BY	0	14400	14400

Challenge the loss in sales. Sales team usually resist price increases.
Note use Contribution analysis not P&L bottom line.

The finance director thinks he can sell the written off obsolete stock of 20K for 10K immediately.	SALES	PROFIT	CASH
Cash received for sale			10000
Written off in P&L so not exist in accounts 100% of PROFIT		10000	
NET POSITION INCREASE PROFIT BY	0	10000	10000

The marketing director wants to engage a consultant for 50K payable in Q1. The consultant expects to increase sales by 25% in the year.	SALES	PROFIT	CASH
Spend guaranteed to be real			
Usually higher due to cost drift and expenses estimate at 55K		-55000	-55000
Extra sales	120000		
Contribution on extra sales at marginal contribution would be 600K x 25% x 52% = 78K.		78000	
Assume all extra contribution in cash in the year?			78000
Add estimated 20K to fixed costs as a 25% increase will impact		-20000	-20000
NET POSITION **INCREASE PROFIT BY**	120000	3000	3000

What is your confidence level?
What are the long term implications on profit, costs and payback?

The major customer that comprises 30% of the sales has agreed to pay in the month if we provide a 2% prompt payment discount.	SALES	PROFIT	CASH
Cost to business is 2% of 30% of Sales = 600K x 30% x 2% =		-3600	
All cash			-3600
Cash increases by 30 days for this business = 180K / 12 =			15000
NET POSITION **REDUCE PROFIT INCREASE CASH**	0	-3600	11400

Do you need the cash that badly?
Will other customers want same?
Can you negotiate lower %?
What is cost of money to business?

The Finance director wants to tell all suppliers that terms are now 60 days not 30 days.	SALES	PROFIT	CASH
No P&L impact	0	0	
Extra 30 Days for materials in CREDITORS			25000
Maybe extra 60 days for other items. Estimate 80% success??			20000
NET POSITION **INCREASE CASH ONLY**	0	0	45000

Do you need the cash that badly?
Will suppliers just increase prices?
Will the suppliers cooperate?

For 20 customers with sales of 50K the income price covers the **DIRECT COSTS ONLY** plus 3K the finance director wants to double the prices for these 20 customers. The sales director thinks half of these customers will be lost at the proposed new prices.	SALES	PROFIT	CASH
Lose all existing trading 20 customers sales of 50K Cost of Materials 47K Contribution 3K	-50000	-3000	-3000
Double prices of 10 customers left sales now 25K x 2	50000		
Contribution is all the increased price 25K plus half the original profit (3/2) 1.5K		26500	
All the contribution will go to CASH			26500
NET POSITION INCREASE PROFIT BY	0	23500	23500

This works well, but only in the margin of the few bad customers.
Make sure there are no independencies between customers.

The manufacturing director wants to buy a new machine for 250K. Depreciation will be over 5 years. Labor costs are expected to be reduced by 20%, but improved quality.	SALES	PROFIT	CASH
Cost of machine on lease say for 5 years would be 50K PA			-50000
Labor savings each year projected at 20% of 90K		18000	18000
Depreciation entry each year on P&L		-50000	
NET POSITION REDUCE PROFIT BY	0	-32000	-32000

What **OTHER** benefits can be identified?
Would you want this level of debt on the balance sheet?

The buyer wants to source 50% of the material from off-shore at a 20% cost saving. The supply chain is considered risky so he also proposes that the inventory is increased to hold an extra 3 months.	SALES	PROFIT	CASH
Savings on material purchases is 20% x 50% of the 200K spend.		20000	20000
Extra Inventory would be 25% (3 months) value 25K service charge for cash at 3%		-750	-750
NET POSITION INCREASE PROFIT BY	0	19250	19250

Are the numbers real?
Extra costs are required to support an international supply chain?
Will the quality be acceptable?
How do the cash flows work? Duty? Freight? Insurance?
Obsolescence risk due to higher inventory extended supply chain.

THIS QUESTION IS SO IMPORTANT THAT A WHOLE PAGE HAS BEEN ALLOCATED TO IT.

The operations director wants to run a 1% improvement program on ALL activities of the business. Would you support that? What would the likely return be as a % to NET Profit?

Turn page to see likely outcome!

1% PROFIT IMPROVEMENT EXERCISE

Most businesses are reasonably well managed, and there is little low-hanging fruit or obvious areas for savings. Improvements often have to be achieved through a continuous improvement program to achieve single digit upsides. If we take the profit and loss account for the business on P17 and apply a 1% improvement across the board, the results are surprisingly good. See the example below.

PROFIT AND LOSS ACCOUNT STARTING NUMBERS			PROFIT AND LOSS ACCOUNT with 1% improvement	
	SALES	600000	SALES	606000
COST OF SALES			COST OF SALES	
DIRECT LABOR	90000		DIRECT LABOR	89100
MATERIALS	200000		MATERIALS	198000
ALLOCATED OVERHEADS	120000		ALLOCATED OVERHEADS	118800
SCRAPPED MATERIAL	5000		SCRAPPED MATERIAL	4950
SUB TOTAL	415000		SUB TOTAL	410850
	GROSS MARGIN	185000 / 30.8%	GROSS MARGIN	195150 / 32.2%
OVERHEADS			OVERHEADS	
RENT	20000		RENT	20000
INTEREST	3000		INTEREST	3000
SUNDRY EXPENSES	25000		SUNDRY EXPENSES	24750
ADMIN PAYROLL	30000		ADMIN PAYROLL	29700
STOCK WRITE OFF	20000		STOCK WRITE OFF	19800
OBSOLETE STOCK PROV	30000		OBSOLETE STOCK PROV	29700
BAD DEBT PROVISION	15000		BAD DEBT PROVISION	15000
SUB TOTAL	143000		SUB TOTAL	141950
	NET PROFIT	42000 / 7.0%	NET PROFIT	53200 / 8.8%

% PROFIT IMPROVEMENT 26.7%

PROFIT CALCULATION

INCREASED SALES	6000	
MATERIAL SAVING	2000	ORIG PROFIT 42000
LAB SAVING	900	EXTRA PROFIT 11200
PRO OVERHEADS SAVED	1200	NEW PROFIT 53200
REDUCED SCRAP	50	*INCREASE* 26.7%
ADMIN OVERHEADS SAVED	1050	
TOTAL	11200 EXTRA PROFIT	

PROFIT = CASH?

In the ideal world PROFIT should equal CASH; in the real world it usually does not. It is VERY IMPORTANT to RECONCILE DIFFERENCES.

INCORRECT COSTING STANDARDS CAN ACCOUNT FOR WHY CASH DOES NOT EQUAL PROFIT

GOOD REASONS FOR MORE CASH THAN PROFIT
Down cycle releasing cash as inventory depleted
Collect debts (payables) faster
Extending creditors (make sure not too much)
Business financing / Investment / Bank loan / Cash injection

GOOD REASONS FOR LESS CASH THAN PROFIT
Growth, increased inventory, investment
Paying off debt
Up-front payments at a discount

BAD REASONS FOR MORE CASH THAN PROFIT
Inventory levels too low to service customers
Failing business releasing inventory, operating costs being removed

BAD REASONS FOR LESS CASH THAN PROFIT
Poor inventory management
Inefficient operations / Scrap
General mismanagement
Fraud / Dishonesty
Poor debt collection performance

A LONG TERM DIFFERENCE BETWEEN CASH AND PROFIT THE SAME WAY USUALLY MEANS A BIG PROBLEM. FIND IT !

BREAK EVEN CHARTS

NOTES ON BREAK EVEN CHARTS

THESE CHARTS ARE NOT AS WIDELY USED AS THEY USED TO BE.
THEY DO HOWEVER PROVIDE AN IMMEDIATE VISUAL
REPRESENTATION ABOUT A BUSINESS
IN PARTICULAR THEY CLEARLY ILLUSTRATE THE RELATIONSHIP
BETWEEN FIXED AND VARIABLE COSTS

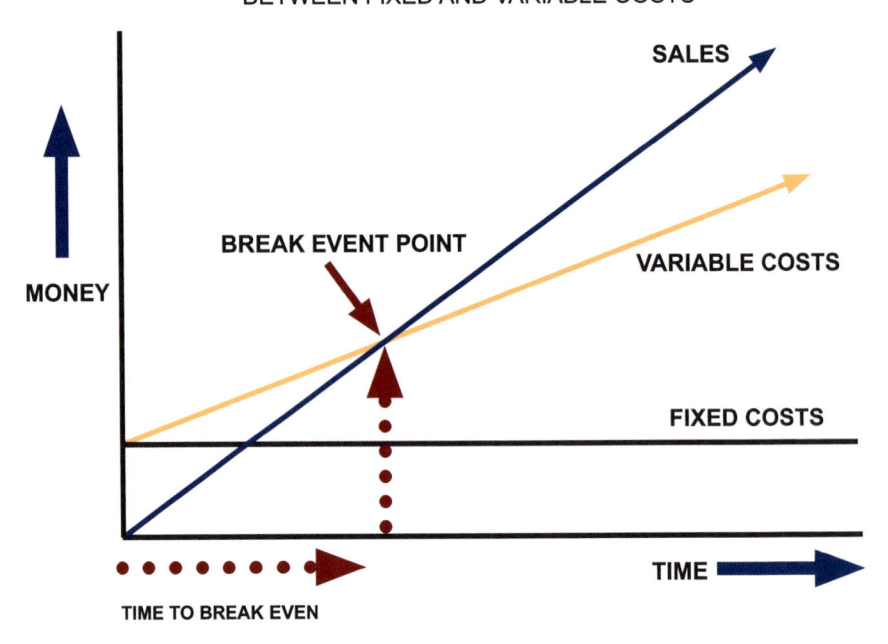

MONEY

SALES

BREAK EVENT POINT

VARIABLE COSTS

FIXED COSTS

TIME

TIME TO BREAK EVEN

EXAMPLES OF TWO DIFFERENT COMPANIES

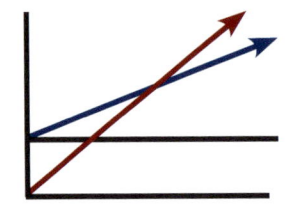

HIGH FIXED COSTS
LONG TIME TO BREAK EVEN
COST CONTROL REQUIRED ON FIXED COSTS
LOOK TO REDUCE COST BASE
HIGH PURCHASED GOODS
CONTROLS REQUIRED

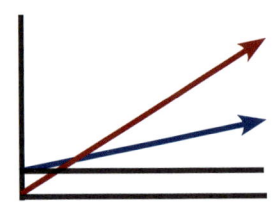

LOW COST BASE HIGH MARGIN PRODUCT
FOCUS ON MAX SALES AND VOLUME
DISCOUNTING / MARGINAL COSTING OPPORTUNITIES

PROFIT — WHAT IS IT?

A THOUGHT

PROFIT is one of the most widely used words in the business world and indeed in the outside world, as well. It is usually used to refer to a GAIN of some form. Yet you cannot see it, you cannot touch it, and if you were asked to show it to someone, you would be unable to do so. I find it interesting that so much effort goes into what could be considered a nebulous concept.

WHAT IS IT?

It is the difference between two things that you can definitely identify. The difference between income and expenditure. Plus the change in the value of any assets or liabilities.

HOW IS PROFIT CREATED?

Two ways. First make sure that INCOME exceeds expenditure, and secondly make sure that the ASSETS increase in value.

THE POINT

Whenever talking about PROFIT, especially PROFIT IMPROVEMENT, identify the best areas where this can be achieved. The options:

INCREASE INCOME

REDUCE EXPENDITURE

INCREASE THE VALUE OF ASSETS

REDUCE THE VALUE / COST OF LIABILITIES

See the "A Day With a CEO Handbook" for over 100 ideas on how to improve profitability.

COSTING SYSTEMS

PURPOSE OF A COSTING SYSTEM

The traditional main accounts — P&L, CASH FLOW and BALANCE SHEET — are of course important and would be viewed as part of the FINANCIAL ACCOUNTING requirements of the business. Accountants often differentiate their activities by calling all the more management and cost related reporting MANAGEMENT ACCOUNTING. Of course in the final analysis it is all management accounting, but the management of costing systems is typically carried out by the management accountants as they are expected to be more directly involved in the DAY-TO-DAY business analyzing the TRANSACTIONS and EXPENSES. These detailed transactions are best tracked by a COSTING SYSTEM that CHECKS if they are PROFITABLE TRANSACTIONS.

AN OPINION

If you understand the relationship between fixed and variable costs, see break even charts on page 25, and you understand the concepts of absorption costing and you also understand the way a costing system interacts with the three main financial accounts, then you have all that you require to understand any costing system and evaluate its strengths and weaknesses. More importantly you will have the tools to choose or develop a costing system entirely suited to your business. You could forward an argument that most costing systems are a variation of ABSORPTION COSTING it is just a matter of degree. Typically the more STANDARD products or hours that you sell the more absorbed will be the standard cost rates and the more that this type of business would use STANDARD COSTS. The more fragmented and variable, or one off your product and services are the more you will use the more bespoke VARIABLE COSTING approach. Some names that cover this approach ACTIVITY COSTING, PROJECT COSTING.

ABSORPTION COSTING

This is the most common system as it enables many of the OVERHEADS in addition to the DIRECT SPEND to be included in one ABSORBED COST RATE, which can be easily used at the point of sale and all wrapped up in the one price. The other aspect of ABSORPTION COSTING is that as a result of using the full cost standards it may be that **SOME** of the **PROFIT IS TAKEN EARLY AND HELD IN INVENTORY.** This is an opportunity but can result is many problems.

THIS BOOK FOCUSES ON ABSORPTION COSTING
DUE TO ITS WIDESPREAD USE AND IMPORTANCE.
AN UNDERSTANDING OF ABSORPTION COSTING WILL COVER MOST OPTIONS.

SUPER SIZE THE FRIES?

MARKETING IDEA

The story goes that David Wallerstein a cinema owner in the Midwest of America in the 1960s was struggling to make a profit, so he had this idea that when someone purchased a soda and popcorn he would offer to double them for half the price. It was a great success and this simple concept is now in widespread use in business, especially in the fast food industry. A great success if you ignore the obesity and diabetes arguments!

BUSINESS LANGUAGE

David realized that once the original sale had been committed and the customer was captive that the initial purchase would cover the overheads on an absorbed basis, therefore he could now apply a marginal costing technique whereby any extra revenue after it covered the cost of the extra food would go to profit. He could UPSELL at a lower price and make more money. A spectacularly effective example of how an understanding of absorption costing and the application of marginal costing created more profit and probably saved the business.

THE REQUIREMENT

ABSORPTION COSTING is in widespread use in most businesses and an understanding of how it works will create opportunities to improve the profitability of the business. A failure to understand can get you into a whole lot of trouble very quickly and in some instances cause a business to fail.

The next few pages are heavy going, but essential reading for a GM, as in my experience one of the most common weaknesses I have observed in an executive is a failure to fully understand ABSORPTION costing and consequently to not appreciate the opportunities and dangers.

ABSORPTION COSTING — THE THEORY

How often have you heard in a bar how disgraceful it is to charge for a drink much more than the same drink costs in the local grocery store? The bar owner would say that the difference between the costs when they pay for the drink versus what they are charging their customers is not all profit. The selling price also has to cover all the overheads of the bar.

THE REASON ABSORPTION COSTING IS USED IS BECAUSE IT MAKES IT SIMPLE AT THE POINT OF SALE TO INCLUDE OVERHEADS INTO ONE UNIT PRICE.

If we take a simple example that a bar sold 1000 drinks a month and that they were purchased for $1 each and that the **OVERHEAD** costs were $3000 per month, the **ABSORPTION COSTING PROCESS** would be as follows.

Note the basic terminology that anyone in a business that uses absorption costing will use. Using the numbers from the BAR example.

PRIME or DIRECT COST — This is the external spend per transaction. In this instance it is the cost of buying the drink, $1.

OVERHEADS TO BE ABSORBED — This is a calculation made by the accountants / managers as to what items will go into the calculation of the absorbed rate per unit of sale. In this instance 1000 DRINKS. It may not include all the overheads in the business, just those related to the activity that the sale is the **DIRECTLY RELATED OVERHEADS**. For example, in this bar it may include: bar payroll, heating, cleaning, consumables like nuts, etc. **In this example it is $3000.** It would probably not include the Sales and General Administrative expenses (SG&A), which are $500.

ABSORBED STANDARD UNIT COST — This will be the amount of overhead recovered per item of sale. In this instance, per drink. This is calculated by dividing the total **OVERHEADS TO BE ABSORBED** by the **UNIT SALES**. $3,000 to be recovered over 1,000 drinks is $3 per drink.

UNIT FULLY ABSORBED COST — The unit cost is made up of the **DIRECT SPEND**, plus the **OVERHEAD ABSORBED UNIT COST**. The unit cost is the cost of buying the drink $1, plus the overhead rate $3, giving a **UNIT COST** of $4.

ABSORPTION COSTING — THE THEORY

UNIT SELLING PRICE — When the cost has been calculated, then someone has to determine the **UNIT SELLING PRICE**. This should always be based on what the market will accept, ***NOT A FORMULAE BASED ON THE UNIT COST*** (which it often is). Therefore, if the bar owner thinks they can sell the drink for $6, that is the **UNIT SELLING PRICE**.

MARGIN (GROSS) — The profit margin on the sale is the difference between the **UNIT SELLING PRICE** and the **UNIT FULLY ABSORBED COST**. In this example it is the $6 sales price less the $4, giving $2 Gross Profit of 33% (2/6 as a % calculation).

CONTRIBUTION — The contribution is the amount that each drink contributes to the running of the business. That is the difference between the **UNIT SELLING PRICE** (income) and **DIRECT EXTERNAL COSTS** (money out the business). For this example, the contribution is **UNIT SALES PRICE ($6)** less the **DIRECT COSTS ($1)** equals **$5 CONTRIBUTION**.

GRAPHIC REPRESENTATION

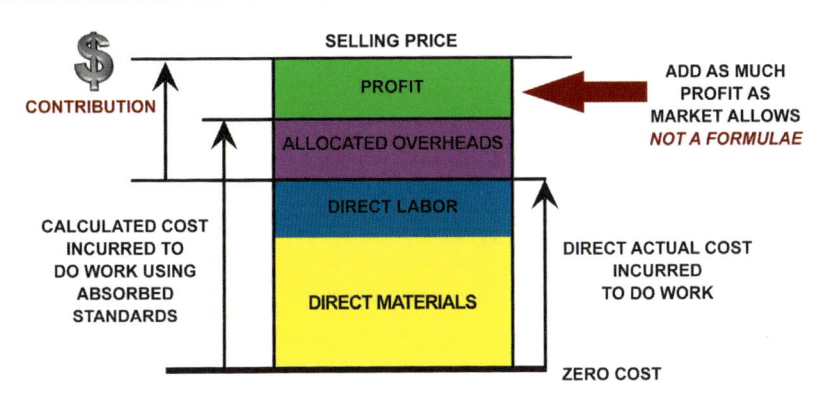

NOTE: The graphic includes more typically DIRECT LABOR and DIRECT MATERIAL.

So far so good, all very simple and most managers get this and understand it.

OVER AND UNDER ABSORPTION

THE ISSUE

I have labored the point in great detail because I will now explain why absorption costing is full of potential pitfalls and also opportunities. This is very important as I have seen so many situations where a lack of understanding of the ABSORPTION COSTING process has caused problems and in some instances business failure. Because there has been an over dependence upon the simplicity of the process. Managers can quickly grasp the concept of selling a drink for $6 with a 33% margin and that is often all they are advised. (There are good arguments for keeping it that way, which will come out in the following analysis.) The standards that are often carved in stone and used widely in the day-to-day activities of a business for estimating and invoicing etc. are based on two ESTIMATES— that the bar will sell 1000 drinks and that the actual costs will be $3000. (I will ignore the ability to achieve the sales price in this exercise, but it is of course fundamentally important.) If these two assumptions are not achieved then this leads to OVER or UNDER ABSORPTION. This is the root cause of many problems and is illustrated and explained on the next few pages.

EXAMPLES (P&L ACCOUNT OPPOSITE)

A — **ON PLAN**
The bar achieves the forecast and all costs are as expected. A nominal $500 has been included for Sales and General Admin. expenses, (SG&A)

B — **UNDER ABSORBED**
The bar sells 800 drinks, not the planned 1000.
All other costs remain as forecast

C — **OVER ABSORBED**
The bar sells 1200 drinks, not the planned 1000.
All other costs remain as forecast

NOTE:
Under absorbed by 200 drinks results in a 10.4% PROFIT (B)
Over absorbed by 200 drinks results in a 34.7% PROFIT (C)

PROFIT AND LOSS IMPACTS WITH OVER /UNDER ABSORPTION

ACTUAL SALES SAME AS PLAN   **1000** $ **A**

SALES	($6 X 1000)		6000
COST OF SALES			
DIRECT COSTS	($1 X 1000)	1000	
RECOVERED OVERHEADS	($3 X 1000)	3000	
	(3000 RECOVERED)		
TOTAL COST OF SALES			4000
GROSS MARGIN			2000 **33.3%**
SG & A		500	
NET PROFIT			**1500** **25.0%**

ACTUAL SALES 200 BELOW PLAN   **800** $ **B**

SALES	($6 X 800)		4800
COST OF SALES			
DIRECT COSTS	($1 X 800)	-800	
RECOVERED OVERHEADS	($3 X 800)	-2400	
UNDER RECOVERED OVERHEADS	**(3000-2400)**	**-600**	
TOTAL COST OF SALES			-3800
GROSS MARGIN			1000 **20.8%**
SG & A		500	
NET PROFIT			**500** **10.4%**

ACTUAL SALES 200 ABOVE PLAN   **1200** $ **C**

SALES	($6 X 1200)		7200
COST OF SALES			
DIRECT COSTS	($1 X 1200)	-1200	
RECOVERED OVERHEADS	($3 X 1200)	-3600	
OVER RECOVERED OVERHEADS	**(3600 -3000)**	**600**	
TOTAL COST OF SALES			4200
GROSS MARGIN			3000 **41.7%**
SG & A		500	
NET PROFIT			**2500** **34.7%**

ACTIVITIES THAT IMPACT OVER / UNDER RECOVERY

ACTUAL SALES SAME AS PLAN
P&L ACC.   DRINKS **1000** $ **A**

SALES	($6 X 1000)		6000
COST OF SALES			
DIRECT COSTS	($1 X 1000)	1000	
RECOVERED OVERHEADS	($3 X 1000)	3000	
	(3000 RECOVERED)		
TOTAL COST OF SALES			4000
GROSS MARGIN			2000 33.3%
SG & A		500	
NET PROFIT			**1500** 25.0%

SOME POSSIBLE SITUATIONS COMPARED TO A THE BUDGET

Note the different scenarios and how the outcome has been calculated using the CONTRIBUTION and the P&L route.

UPSIDES (Upside profit to plan)	PROFIT IMPACT
Bar team reaches 1000 target and decides to offer discretionary sales at $5 and sells another 300 drinks at this price	PLUS
Costs same and all of the overheads are covered, so EXTRA contribution is $4 ($5 -$1) per drink for an extra 300 drinks equals $1200 UPSIDE	1200
P&L route. Sales $7500 less $3000 overheads less $1300 cost of drinks less $500 SG&A gives profit of $2700 UPSIDE of $1200 to planned profit $1500	1200

ACTIVITIES THAT IMPACT OVER / UNDER RECOVERY

UPSIDES (Upside profit to plan)	PROFIT IMPACT
The owner gives the bar team a bonus scheme that for all drinks that they sell over 1000 they will receive $1 per drink. Bar team sells 1200 drinks all at $6	**PLUS**
Extra contribution is 200 x $5 total $1000 less bonus paid of $200 total UPSIDE profit $800	**800**
P&L route. Sales $7200 less $3000 overheads less $1200 drinks less bonus of $200 less $500 SG&A gives profit of $2300 UPSIDE of $800 to plan profit $1500	**800**

DOWNSIDES (Loss created)	PROFIT IMPACT
Sales are slow and the owner decides to do a two for one happy hour. Sells 500 drinks at $6 and gives 50 drinks away	**LOSS**
Contribution of $2500 (500 x $5) gives under recovered overheads of $500 Which added to the SG&A $500 and the cost of free drinks $50 gives LOSS of $1050	**1050**
P&L route. Sales $3000 less $3000 overheads less $550 drinks less $500 SG&A gives LOSS of $1050	**1050**

BREAK EVEN	PROFIT IMPACT
Sales are slow and the owner decides to do a two for one happy hour. Sells 900 drinks at $6 and gives 100 drinks away	**BREAK EVEN**
Contribution of $4500 (900 x $5) results in $1500 over recovered overheads less SG&A $500 less cost of drinks $1000 gives BREAK EVEN	**0**
P&L route. Sales $7200 less $3000 overheads less $1200 drinks less bonus of 200 less $500 SG&A gives BREAK EVEN	**0**

Why not try a few different ideas of your own and see what the implications are for the P&L. Use both methods to calculate and make sure that you understand the reconciliation.

THE PROBLEM

When the standards have been calculated they are often then used widely in the organization with a sense of certainty, often innocence and usually with a false sense of confidence. They are usually used in the estimating process, which will have a direct impact on **PRICING**. They are maybe used for financial planning cost reviews, incentive setting and calculations. In short, they are usually at the heart of the costing system.

This all inclusive RATE is based on some major assumptions, most notably that the volumes will be met and the actual costs are as budgeted. If you add product mix and price erosion, then the probability of the standards fully reflecting the actuals on an ongoing and dynamic basis is low. So the question therefore is, how much will the difference be and which way will the difference go? Too large a downside and a nasty surprise in the accounts and maybe you have been working for little profit. The "Busy Fools Syndrome." If you have an upside or over recovery, great! Maybe a windfall profit through extra volume, but have you missed some marginal costing opportunities by using higher than required prices?

Unfortunately these differences are virtually impossible to detect in real time due to the complexity of most businesses and the way that the inventory is calculated and checked. You normally only get to find out after the accounts have been closed and the inventory reconciled. Maybe you have to wait for a physical count?

THE OPPORTUNITY (Marginal costing)

Many businesses use absorbed rates to quote for work or to sell products. The local garage repairing a car for $60 / hour. Restaurants marking food up in the menu, professional services, such as accountants and lawyers charging by the hour, etc.

All of these rates are based on a base load of expected basic hours from which to recover the overheads. An example. A machinist sells his time by the STANDARD COST PER HOUR at $150 per hour based on a standard hourly COST RATE of $100 marked up 50% for profit (to give $150) the numbers being based on a nominal 40 hour week and includes the ACTUAL DIRECT COST of the person at $20 / hour resulting in a CONTRIBUTION of $130 ($80 overhead contribution plus $50 profit) per hour sold. For the first 40 hours charged the $80 contribution will cover the overhead. On any hours over the base load of 40 as the overheads have been recovered the additional hours that are sold over the 40 only have to recover the incremental ACTUAL UNIT COST of working those extra hours. If for the example the machinist is prepared to work for $30 per hour overtime and maybe direct consumable will cost $5 per hour then the cost to the business of delivering that extra hour is $35 ($30 plus $5). If that hour is now sold at any price over $35 then the extra revenue will go straight into profit (and cash) so for example if the sales person wants to maintain the 50% mark up to sales then the price would be $52.5 (35 x 1.5) if the sales person wants to maintain the actual $50 per hour profit then the selling price will be $85. ($35 + $50) / hour. The super sales person will of course sell for the $150 plus a mark up for overtime working and make SUPER PROFITS.
(For example if the price is marked up for overtime by 50% the selling price is $225 (150 + 75) / hour and the total CONTRIBUTION AND PROFIT is $190 / hour ($225 -$35). Note that when planned volume has been achieved then the overheads are fully recovered CONTRIBUTION AND PROFIT are the same!

THE BIG PROBLEM — INVENTORY VALUATION LOSSES

The way absorption costing impacts the valuation of inventory is fundamental.

This is where the UNDER ABSORBED issues usually show up. An example:

A business purchases some raw material from which it is planned to manufacture 50 components. If the material costs $1000, it is taken into inventory at $1000. The raw material is taken from inventory and machined into 50 pieces and this will take 20 hours at a standard cost of $100 per hour. So these parts are now worth the $1000 cost of raw material, plus the $2000 of added value that has been added in the manufacturing process. These parts are finished and go to the finished inventory at a value of $3000 ($1000 plus 20 x $100 / hour). Parts would show in inventory at $60 each ($3000 / 50). The sales price per part is $100. The inventory would be valued at $3000.

Given that the auditors have also verified the following:

>   The business is an ongoing viable concern.

>   The accounting standards are still in line with reality.

>   The parts have not been in inventory a long time and have to be written down as per the obsolescence policy.

>   The parts are there after a physical count and fit for sale.

>   The expected sales value is greater than the $60 cost.

THE BIG PROBLEM — INVENTORY VALUATION LOSSES

If all of these AUDIT tests are passed, then the valuation is accepted. The important point is that these parts now effectively include a CONTRIBUTION TO PROFIT, which has already been taken into the book of accounts. For example, if the standard rate of $100 includes $60 of overhead recovery then this is in the finished goods valuation. When an inventory count is taken it is not unusual to have a variance from the book accounts. A physical count is therefore about reconciling all these COSTING variabilities and not just about counting the parts as they have overheads attached. So why do differences occur?

Overbooking of hours due to inefficiency.

Scrapped product not booked.

Creeping obsolescence.

Standards changed.

Processes changed on shop floor and wrong standards used.

Over production to order and surplus product not saleable.

Inefficiencies not reported.

Shop floor booking system not good enough.

Operator error booking wrong job wrong hours.

Pay attention! This is a huge area for problems and surprises!

TO RE-CAP

Before we get into some heavy lifting with a more detailed ABSORPTION COSTING exercise, it is worth a re-cap on the essential features of this type of costing system using what is a very simple example using the drinks bar with just one product, one price and no complications. However, even in this example you should recognize three major components that a GM heeds to be aware of in the design and operation of an ABSORPTION COSTING system.

DESIGN OF THE SYSTEM
What goes into the rate calculation?
How many rates do you use?
How do you fix the selling **PRICE?**

HOW ACTUAL PERFORMANCE CHANGES IMPACT P&L
Do you understand the impact of sales variances?
How to treat over and under recoveries?

THE ACTIVITIES OF PEOPLE CAN IMPACT RESULTS
What do you tell your team?
Do you trust them to operate a marginal costing system?
What controls would you put in for estimating / pricing?

Just consider that even in this simple example issues that require the judgment of a GM are involved. Now project these principles into a much larger organization with maybe thousands of products and people, customers plus inventory and a complicated supply and distribution channels. This complex situation will be very difficult to understand and manage especially in a real time situation. As a result issues normally only become apparent after a physical inventory count, which may be well after the point of control. The GM therefore needs to understand the issues that could impact that inventory valuation and try to anticipate outcomes. Easier said than done, but try to get in front of these issues by understanding the characteristics of the costing systems and what opportunities and risks, upsides and downsides are inherent.

The final point to make is that these concepts apply to a multitude of businesses in many sectors, a bar has been used to demonstrate the concept and a manufacturing company example has been used for a more detailed example, but the points behind these two examples apply to so many businesses. For example, service companies charging by the hour, such as retail stores and restaurants.

ABSORPTION COSTING

A DETAILED EXERCISE

The next few pages show a detailed exercise for a machining business, typical of the many thousands of manufacturing plants throughout the world. It is a very simple example to illustrate the concepts. If you do understand what is in here, then it will enable you to review the larger, more complex situations with confidence.

ABSORPTION COSTING EXERCISE WITH NUMBERS. BASED UPON A MACHINING COMPANY WITH DATA AS BELOW

THE BUSINESS

MACHINE SHOP

THIS EXERCISE IS FOR ONE ACCOUNTING PERIOD.

TOTAL HOURS AVAILABLE (BASIC WORKING IN ACCOUNTING PERIOD)	1000
NUMBER OF MACHINE OPERATORS	6
BASIC HOURLY PAY OF EACH OPERATOR	10
SO TOTAL LABOR HOURS ARE (6 X 1000)	6000
TOTAL DIRECT LABOR COST IS (6000 X 10)	60000
TOTAL NUMBER OF MACHINES AVAILABLE ARE	8
TOTAL MACHINE HOURS AVAILABLE ARE (8 X 1000)	8000

PRODUCTION OVERHEADS ARE

MACHINE DEPRECIATION	240000
FIXED FACTORY COSTS	120000
MACHINE CONSUMABLES	48000
PRODUCTION SUPERVISION AND PLANNING	24000

BUSINESS OVERHEADS (S,G & A)

1 GENERAL MANAGER	60000
QUALITY COSTS	62000
SALES COSTS	40000
SITE HQ OVERHEADS	84000
	246000

NOTES
OVERTIME AVAILABLE UP TO 2000 HOURS PER PERIOD
SOME OPERATORS CAN WORK UP TO 3 MACHINES
OVERTIME PAID AT TIME PLUS 50% (15 PER HOUR)

Quality costs may sometimes be included in the direct rate calculation if high.

FROM THIS BASIC DATA WE CAN CALCULATE THE STANDARD COST RATES TO BE USED

CALCULATION OF RATES

CONCEPTUAL CONSIDERATIONS

To determine what rates are to be used in an ABSORPTION COSTING system, two basic judgments are required.

FIRST
What is the base unit for the rate calculation? Typically either LABOR HOURS and / or MACHINE HOURS

SECOND
What costs are to be included into the rate calculation to be allocated to the units selected in the first question?

The question is how to use as few rates as possible that accurately reflect the realistic costs of the business. So for example, in a labor-intensive business where time is sold then an HOURLY RATE is fine. For capital-intensive business with low overhead costs a MACHINE HOUR RATE or an uplift of the raw material intake is maybe fine. For a hybrid with several machines and considerable labor involved then an HOURLY RATE **AND** A MACHINE RATE is probably the best option. In all scenarios, pay attention to what is going into the lump sum overheads before they are allocated. Be aware of the requirement to review and change as required.

AN EXAMPLE OF CHANGING SITUATIONS

A machine shop working in the medical devices industry included the cost of shop floor quality inspectors in the overheads to calculate the machine hour rate. Quality regulations and customer demands increased over a couple of years to the point that it was taking more hours to inspect a part than to make it. Inspection costs were increasing and not proportionally loaded to the differing requirements of customers. The result was that considerable under recoveries were being reported. Action was to create a separate QUALITY HOUR RATE, which was used in the quotation process, and that was visible to customers and mainly understood and accepted by them and the result was that the margins increased. A profit improvement result generated by watching the standard absorbed rate calculations.

CALCULATION OF ABSORBED RATES TO BE USED

STEP 1
Decide that all the "BUSINESS OVERHEADS" are excluded and they will go DIRECTLY into the P&L account.

STEP 2
Calculate the cost per MACHINE HOUR.

		RATE / HOUR
Total machine hours	8000	
DEPRECIATION	240000	30
MACHINE CONSUMABLES	48000	6
MACHINE HOURLY RATE		**36**

STEP 3
Calculate the cost per LABOR HOUR.

Total labor hours	6000	
PAY LABOR PER HOUR	60000	10
FIXED FACTORY COSTS	120000	20
PRODUCTION SUPERVISION AND PLANNING	24000	4
LABOR HOURLY RATE		**34**

THESE TWO RATES COULD BE USED TOGETHER AND WILL BE USED IN THIS EXERCISE

ALTERNATIVE
Maybe put everything into ONE LABOR RECOVERY RATE

EXAMPLE

Total labor hours	6000	
PAY LABOR PER HOUR	60000	10
FIXED FACTORY COSTS	120000	20
PRODUCTION SUPERVISION AND PLANNING	24000	4
DEPRECIATION	240000	40
MACHINE CONSUMABLES	48000	8
ALL COST LABOR HOURLY RATE		**82**

ESTIMATING JOBS USING THESE RATES
THE BUSINESS HAS 3 JOBS AND THEY HAVE BEEN ESTIMATED AS FOLLOWS

We will be using **TWO** rates because there are a different number of machines to operators.
The use of two rates should more realistically recover the cost for the machine when one operator is running more than one machine.
For simplicity we will presume that this company only has THREE JOBS.

JOB	PURCHASED DIRECT MATERIAL	NUMBER OPERATORS	LABOR HOURS	NUMBER MACHINES	MACHINE HOURS
A	600000	3	3000	5	5000
B	100000	2	2000	2	2000
C	1000	1	1000	1	1000
TOTALS	701000	6	6000	8	8000

KEY POINTS
GOOD ESTIMATING IS THE KEY TO A GOOD RESULT.
A POOR ESTIMATE YOU ARE BUILDING ON SAND.
CHECK ACTUAL COSTS WHEN JOB IS CLOSED.
MOST COMPANIES HAVE MANY MORE JOBS.

NEXT STAGE
THESE ESTIMATES ARE USED WITH THE CALCULATED HOURLY RATES TO PRODUCE A FULL FINANCIAL ESTIMATE AS SHOWN ON P44.

JOB ESTIMATES *FINANCIAL WORK UP USING RATES AND ESTIMATES*

JOB REF	A	B	C	TOTAL
DIRECT MATERIAL	600000	100000	1000	701000
MATERIAL MARK UP				
LABOR HOURS	3000	2000	1000	6000
ABSORBED RATE	34	34	34	
LABOR COST	102000	68000	34000	204000
MACHINE HOURS	5000	2000	1000	8000
ABSORBED RATE	36	36	36	
MACHINE COST	180000	72000	36000	288000
TOTAL COST	882000	240000	71000	1193000

At this stage a decision is required as to what *PROFIT* to add by *UPLIFTING THE RATES*. A *MARKETING DECISION* is made to add 70% to the Labor and Machine hourly costs.

PROFIT UPLIFT	197400	98000	49000	344400 NOTE 2
	This then gives the selling price.			
SELLING PRICE	1079400	338000	120000	1537400
				TOTAL SALES
GROSS MARGIN	18.3%	29.0%	40.8%	22.4%

FROM THESE ESTIMATES WE ARE ABLE TO CALCULATE THE TOTAL SALES AND THE MATERIAL SPEND WE CAN NOW CALCULATE THE PROFIT & LOSS ACCOUNT, P45

NOTE: By marking up the Labor and Material by 70% The resulting rates for use in future ESTIMATING would be.

	BASE	MARK UP	NEW RATE
LABOR	34	23.8	57.8
MACHINE	36	25.2	61.2

MATERIAL NOT MARKED UP TO KEEP SIMPLE WOULD RECOMMEND MARK UP SAY 10% FOR SCRAP, etc.

PROFIT AND LOSS ACCOUNTS

USING THE INFORMATION FROM THE CALCULATION ON PAGE 44 AND THE BASE DATA ON PAGE 40 WE CAN CONSTRUCT A TYPICAL PROFIT AND LOSS ACCOUNT

P&L ACCOUNT USING PRIME NUMBERS

SALES	1537400
DIRECT MATERIAL SPEND	701000
DIRECT LABOR COST	60000
MACHINE DEPRECIATION	240000
MACHINE CONSUMABLES	48000
FACTORY FIXED OVERHEADS	120000
PRODUCTION FOREMAN PLANNING	24000
TOTAL PRODUCTION COSTS	1193000
GROSS MARGIN	344400 NOTE 2
	22.4%
BUSINESS OVERHEADS (SG & A)	
1 GENERAL MANAGER	60000
QUALITY COSTS	62000
SALES COSTS	40000
SITE HQ OVERHEADS	84000
	246000
NET PROFIT	98400
	6.4%

The account below shows how the P&L may be expressed using ABSORPTION COSTING. All the Production overheads above the Gross Margin would be included in the standards which would then be used to calculate cost of sales. At the planning stage no variance would exist due to OVER / UNDER absorption. When the actuals come through the OVER / UNDER ABSORPTION would be shown on the line indicated.

P&L ACCOUNT USING STANDARD COSTING

SALES	1537400
COST OF SALES USING STANDARDS TO CALCULATE	1193000
UNDER / OVER RECOVERY	0
TOTAL PRODUCTION COSTS	1193000
GROSS MARGIN	344400
	22.4%
BUSINESS OVERHEADS (SG & A)	246000
NET PROFIT	98400
	6.4%

CONTRIBUTION ANALYSIS

JOB REF	A	B	C	TOTAL
SALES AS ESTIMATED	1079400	338000	120000	1537400
PAGE 44				
LESS				
DIRECT COST / CASH OUT ITEMS				
DIRECT MATERIAL	600000	100000	1000	701000
LABOR HOURS	3000	2000	1000	6000
ACTUAL RATE	10	10	10	
LABOR COST / PAYROLL BILL	30000	20000	10000	60000
MACHINE HOURS	5000	2000	1000	8000
ACTUAL RATE	6	6	6	
	30000	12000	6000	48000
DIRECT ACTUAL CASH COST	660000	132000	17000	809000
% OF SALES	61.1%	39.1%	14.2%	
EQUALS TOTAL CONTRIBUTION	419400	206000	103000	728400
	38.9%	60.9%	85.8%	47.4%
CONTRIBUTION IS FROM				
PROFIT UPLIFT	197400	98000	49000	344400
	18.3%	29.0%	40.8%	22.4%
OVERHEAD RECOVERY	222000	108000	54000	464600
	20.6%	32.0%	45.0%	30.2%
SALES	1079400	338000	120000	1537400 TOTAL SALES
GROSS MARGIN	18.3%	29.0%	40.8%	22.4%

ABSORPTION COSTING

QUICK CHECK

PROFIT RECONCILIATION

DID YOU UNDERSTAND

WHY

THE PROFIT ADDED ON SCHEDULE P44 NOTE 2 344000

IS THE SAME AS

THE GROSS MARGIN IN THE P&L ACCOUNT ON P45

QUESTION

WILL THAT ALWAYS BE THE SAME?

ANSWER

ONLY AT PLANNING STAGE,
OPERATIONALLY PROBABLY NOT.

P44 IS A TARGET
P45 WILL BE ADJUSTED FOR OVER / UNDER RECOVERIES.

ABSORPTION COSTING

STRATEGIC OPPORTUNITIES

A few ideas to point the way to find ways of improving the business profitability

BUDGETING

Build contingencies into the standards. Waste / Scrap / etc.

Do not use all available hours in standard calculation (another contingency).

Understand the key assumptions / weak areas. Watch for them.

Develop a KEY ACTION plan to support the budget

BUSINESS OPERATION

Monitor key components volume / cost. Anticipate surprises.

Run cost to complete reports.

Review closed job reports.

Review quote actives. If lost, see if on price. Compare its "contribution."

Make sure standards produce comparative pricing.

Look for marginal costing opportunities when capacity high.

Make sure sales / estimating team trained and controlled.

Look for opportunities beware of problems

BOOKS CLOSED

Normally too late, but?

Review inventory, physical check results.

Review any post-closure adjustments, make sure that you agree.

Review valuation criteria for obsolete stock / valuation changes.

Try and sell any stock declared obsolete before accounts published.

Talk to accountants / auditors and ask what adjustments made. Agree?

Accountants are ultra conservative but can be persuaded, maybe?

Understand the difference between fiscal accounting requirements / formal policies and judgmental opinions.

Learn for the next accounting period

CONTRIBUTION

This is the most important word that you need to know about and FULLY UNDERSTAND using any ABSORPTION COSTING SYSTEM. It is not usually reported in the accounts.

DEFINED

It is the difference between the **SALES PRICE** and the **DIRECT CASH BASED COSTS** that are required to make that SALE.

WHY IS IT IMPORTANT

It is the key information that you require to know when making **STRATEGIC PRICING DECISIONS**. Especially when the volumes are variable and the over / under recovery of overheads is volatile.

VOLUME CHANGE IMPACTS
UP BY 1000 HOURS

Scenario 1
Opportunity to do 1000 more hours on a one man one machine. Material is free issued just charge standard rate per hour.
(Labor 57.8 Machine 61.2. Total 119 per hour. Increased sales 119000)

PROFIT AND LOSS ACCOUNT	ORIGINAL	SCENARIO ONE CHANGE	REVISED	CHG %
SALES	1537400	119000	1656400	7.7%
DIRECT MATERIAL SPEND	701000		701000	0.0%
DIRECT LABOR COST	60000	15000	75000	25.0%
MACHINE DEPRECIATION	240000		240000	0.0%
MACHINE CONSUMABLES	48000	6000	54000	12.5%
FACTORY FIXED OVERHEADS	120000		120000	0.0%
PRODUCTION FOREMAN PLANNING	24000		24000	0.0%
TOTAL PRODUCTION COSTS	1193000	21000	1214000	1.8%
GROSS MARGIN	344400		442400	28.5%
	22.4%		26.7%	19.2%
BUSINESS OVERHEADS (SG & A)				
1 GENERAL MANAGER	60000		60000	0.0%
QUALITY COSTS	62000		62000	0.0%
SALES COSTS	40000		40000	0.0%
SITE HQ OVERHEADS	84000		84000	0.0%
	246000		246000	0.0%
NET PROFIT	98400		196400	99.6%
	6.4%		11.9%	

PROFIT CHANGE   + 98000   99.6%

For scenario 1 labor will work overtime at 15 / hour

VOLUME CHANGE IMPACTS
DOWN BY 1000 HOURS

Scenario 2
Customer B reduces job by 1000 hours. (Half sales of 338000 is 169000)

PROFIT AND LOSS ACCOUNT	ORIGINAL	SCENARIO TWO CHANGE	REVISED	CHG %
SALES	1537400	-169000	1368400	-11.0%
DIRECT MATERIAL SPEND	701000	-50000	651000	-90.7%
DIRECT LABOR COST	60000		60000	0.0%
MACHINE DEPRECIATION	240000		240000	0.0%
MACHINE CONSUMABLES	48000	-6000	42000	12.5%
FACTORY FIXED OVERHEADS	120000		120000	0.0%
PRODUCTION FOREMAN PLANNING	24000		24000	0.0%
TOTAL PRODUCTION COSTS	1193000	-56000	1137000	-4.7%
GROSS MARGIN	344400		231400	-32.8%
	22.4%		16.9%	-24.5%
BUSINESS OVERHEADS (SG & A)				
1 GENERAL MANAGER	60000		60000	0.0%
QUALITY COSTS	62000		62000	0.0%
SALES COSTS	40000		40000	0.0%
SITE HQ OVERHEADS	84000		84000	0.0%
	246000		246000	0.0%
NET PROFIT	98400		-14600	
	6.4%		-1.1%	

PROFIT CHANGES to a LOSS   - 113000

For scenario 2, labor still has to be paid the basic 10 / hour
Can REDUCE the machine consumables at 6 per hour is 6000 reduction
DIRECT MATERIAL is halved, so reduced by 50000

ABSORPTION COSTING

THINGS THAT GO WRONG

A real life and <u>true</u> example of how absorption costing can cost a business a lot of money and inhibit innovation and cost improvement.

THE SITUATION

A manufacturing plant for a large multinational OEM machined and finished parts that were then transferred into a group warehouse at a standard cost. All the operations on site used only a labor absorbed rate of approximately $150 / hour. The plant manager had an incentive bonus on hours booked and the plant was actually rated on this basis. Language internally was used like this is a 300000 hour per year plant.
(Crazy, but that is another point!)

THE PROPOSAL

A supplier came up with what they considered to be an excellent cost reduction opportunity. One of the jobs required a forging to be supplied and it was large and very over size and required the OEM to carry out a lot of machining, several hundred hours per week. The supplier offered to produce a forging much closer to the required shape, which would reduce the machine hours. The increased bought in purchase price difference to be paid by the OEM was not that great because it used considerably less of a high cost material. An obvious and huge cost saving to the OEM with only small change costs involved.

THE OUTCOME

The OEM plant manager refused the proposal because it would have reduced his machine load, manpower and machines all status symbols and what he was measured on.

THE POINT

Make sure that the incentive schemes are aligned with the requirements of the business and will deal with a cost improvement that eliminates hours.

YOU GET WHAT YOU PAY FOR

ABSORPTION COSTING

THINGS THAT GO WRONG

A real life and true example of how absorption costing nearly cost a business a lot of money because the GM did not understand about **CONTRIBUTION**.
Created from the labor **COST STANDARDS**.

THE SITUATION

A GM was reviewing all the jobs on the plant and noticed that a $6M per annum job only had a $200K Gross Margin, so he decided to take the job out and tell the customer that they did not want the work. (Increased prices was not an option.)

THE OUTCOME

Fortunately the accountant pointed out that the job was very heavily labor intensive with a **contribution through the overhead recovery standards** of $3M, plus the $200K margin, so if the job was removed the net cost saving in direct spend would have been $2.8M ($6M sales less total contribution of $3.2M) and most of the cost was own labor, which would have to be laid off, which is another huge cost. If the decision to go ahead was confirmed then the GM would have to replace the $3M contribution, lay off a lot of people and also replace the $200K profit. This would only have been a good idea if the $2.8M of cost (Capacity) could have been utilized on more productive work. The work was kept and a cost improvement program introduced. A close call for the GM.
Hidden consequences of a potentially good decision?

THE POINT

When making a strategic decision involving ABSORPTION COSTING, understand what the **FULL CONTRIBUTION** is and the implications of losing it.

ABSORPTION COSTING

WHAT TO TELL SALES

The big and confusing problem is that the **SAME QUESTION** (what price to sell at?) can have **DIFFERENT ANSWERS** depending where you are on the volume curve.

OPTIONS AND ISSUES

Just advise selling price and discount structure possible

This allows little discretion at the point of sale and will require someone to monitor performance with respect to quote activity, the percentage of jobs won, etc. If changes are required, they would be issued to the sales team as required. This means the sales team is tasked to meet sales price and volume only. This may result in the loss of some marginal costing opportunities as the decision is not at the "point of sale."

Advise sales team of full costing structure, inc contribution

Provides the sales team with good discretion and visibility at the "point of sale," so that ideally they are able to track the market and maximize sales and margin. Dangers are that the sales team will go to the lowest price to win work and chase volume. **Not always a good idea**. If this approach is adopted, the controls require to be stronger and the margins / contributions reviewed in as much of a real time basis as possible. This approach uncontrolled is a very quick way to go bust and fill your capacity with low margin work. Make sure the sales team bonuses are not only on **VOLUME, but also MARGIN.**

CASH MANAGEMENT

NO CASH = NO BUSINESS

Only one page specifically allocated to this fundamental subject. But I hope that the message has come across loud and clear in the rest of the book that CASH is the life blood of a business. No cash does mean you go out of business however excellent all the other business attributes maybe. So all I want to do on this page is to give some tips on how to create and conserve cash.

WAYS TO GENERATE / CONSERVE / CREATE CASH

Make sure that you have the TRUE POSITION REPORTED TO YOU

Stop spending it. Controls.

Look at receivables. Collect quicker.

Look at payables. Pay later.

Cancel all automatic payments. If a problem.

Cancel all direct debits. If problem.

Keep good relationships with banks.

Dispose of all surplus assets and equipment.

Lease back major capital items.

Look at all credit notes / Warranty claims.

See what you do for customers FREE, see if chargeable (e.g., freight).

Look at PRICING CONTROLS.

Stop all discretionary spend (e.g., travel).

Look at commission payments. Realistic, value for money?

Look at temporary staff and consultants.

Review any special payments. Overtime, etc.

Can you get any prompt payments for a discount?

BUDGETING / FINANCIAL PLANNING

THE CONCEPT

A budget or financial plan is the preparation of the main financial accounts for a future period in increments considered appropriate. This is usually the preparation of the P&L, cash flow and balance sheet for the next year in quarterly or monthly segments.

THE REQUIREMENT

The detail and supporting material / schedules can be as complicated as you wish to make it. The main schedules would normally be supported by certain information such as at a minimum: Sales forecast / Manpower plan / Capital investment schedule / Key Actions / Risk assessment.

THE PROCESS

A business may have many different processes that they use and find acceptable. My preference is the following process.

Executive meeting to define main strategic objectives.

Sales forecast prepared and reviewed.

Operations team prepare budget on agreed sales forecast.

All departments prepare budgets on agreed sales / operations budget.

Draft full budget prepared and reviewed.

Budget formally accepted.

Update schedules with ACTUAL closing positions. Usually the year end CASH balances.

Supporting schedules finalized and issued.

Note this is an iterative process.

BUDGETING / FINANCIAL PLANNING

POINTS TO NOTE

Define the strategic intent / mission of the business.

Detail plan with the time period that the business is able to change.

Make sure plans / responsibilities / incentives are aligned.

Make the process inclusive. Get managers to own and agree to the numbers. (Not a financial exercise.)

Be realistic.

Be prepared to change.

Flex the plan and do some *what ifs*.

Have a contingency plan.

Develop a list of **KEY ACTIONS** required to execute the plan.

Develop a list of **UPSIDES** to provide confidence on achievement.

Make sure that you have the **CASH AVAILABLE.**

SAVINGS
REAL OR NOT

AN AREA FOR CREATIVE ACCOUNTING AND DELUSION
Especially where Absorption Costing is used

Do the following when determining actual savings:

FOLLOW THE CASH

- If head count is being reduced, ask for names / dates / costs.
- If inter-company transactions are involved, look at net position.
- If hourly rates involved, make sure direct costs not absorbed rates.
- If a contract / job is being eliminated, make sure the **contribution** is understood not just use calculated profit. How will the contribution be replaced.
- If a project is being justified by internal efficiency improvements, make sure using the **direct costs**, not absorbed rates.

Beware of following comments to justify a proposal:

- It means we do not have to recruit anyone else.
- Make sure anyone talking profit understands what it means.
- Using the discounted cost of money (usually this would be so marginal).
- It's in the budget.
- The customer needs us to do it. Why? Are they paying for it?

DEALING WITH THE SALES TEAM

VERY IMPORTANT REASONS WHY YOU SHOULD

The GM is the No. 1 salesman and defines the company.
They talk to customers, listen to them.
They may control pricing, one of the biggest areas to make or lose money in any business.
They usually have to deal with all the problems that the business creates.
They can be expensive and difficult to manage.
They may have a lot of critical data about customers / products / margins.
They may be hard to recruit and retain. Need some love from the GM!

UNDERSTAND HOW THEY THINK

All generalizations are dangerous, but usually the sales team are?

Aggressive and results orientated.
Optimistic.
Proactive.
Comfortable operating alone away from the company.
Motivated by incentives and bonuses.
Have to deal with rejection and failure on a regular basis.

CONSEQUENTLY

Review all sales forecasts in detail; make sure that they are realistic, not understated to make bonus achievement easy or too optimistic due to misplaced enthusiasm. Pages 60 and 61 show some ideas on how to do that.

Make sure that all incentive schemes are in line with company objectives. You will usually get what you pay for. Sales? Margins? New customers? Virtually all incentive schemes have a shelf life and require to reviewed.

Make sure the internal support systems provide correct back up. So many times I have witnessed a highly paid sales person working inside the business doing basic progress chasing for their customers instead of being out developing new customers and markets.

But above all, do get involved in detail with PRICING.

Pages 60 to 63 cover some basic sales / customer related ideas.

REVIEWING A SALES FORECAST

The Sales Director has submitted the following sales forecast to support the budget.

YEAR 2	Q1	Q2	Q3	Q4	TOTAL
Order intake forecast	160000	150000	170000	150000	630000
Sales forecast	150000	150000	150000	150000	600000

The GM asks the following questions and receives the answers as shown

1. Q What is the opening order book / backlog?
   A 200000
2. Q What is the sales phasing of the opening order book / backlog?
   A 70% in Q1 and 30% in Q2
3. Q What % of the orders received in any Q ship in the same Quarter as received?
   A 50%
4. Q When does the balance of this backlog ship?
   A 30 % in following Q and 20% in second Q following
5. Q What is your on time delivery %?
   A 98%
6. Q What in your order book (backlog) is late being delivered (past due)?
   A 100000
7. Q What is your on-time delivery target for this budget year. No past dues at the year end?
   A 100%
8. Q What % of the backlog (not past due) would be accepted by the customers earlier?
   A 50%
9. Q You currently have 3 sales persons. If it was doubled to 6, would the sales double?
   A Always interesting!

What conclusions / Actions would you take after reviewing the position?

REVISED SALES BUDGET
(Taking into account the answers on P60)

SALES FORECAST GENERATED BY ANSWERS TO QUESTIONS							CLOSING
		Q1	Q2	Q3	Q4	TOTAL	BACKLOG
BACKLOG/ORDER BOOK	200000	140000	60000				
Q1 ORDERS	160000	80000	48000	32000		160000	
Q2 ORDERS	150000		75000	45000	30000	150000	
Q3 ORDERS	170000			85000	51000	136000	34000
Q4 ORDERS	150000				75000	75000	75000
TOTALS	830000	220000	183000	162000	156000 521000		109000
ORIGINAL		150000	150000	150000	150000 600000		

NOTES

This is an entirely typical outcome of these numerate questions. Numbers exaggerated for effect.

This would be considered a budget that was "sand bagged." (Slang for too soft.)

The numbers "do not hang together!"

The original submission showed top-level growth.

After questions indicates that the order intake budget probably understated.

The end of year backlog has reduced.

So in effect, the sales team are forecasting for the business to decline.

The original submission of flat sales and increased orders indicates that the business should be growing.

This numerate analysis indicates the exact opposite. Reduced year-end backlog.

ACTIONS

Change the sales forecast / budget. Which way?

Challenge the sales team as to why the order intake has reduced from last year (800k) to this year (630k).

You need to get to the bottom this 21% reduction. Real?

Or are the sales team looking for an easy life and big bonuses?

Increase the production capacity. Depending upon answer to the above questions.

Reduce lead times as a one-time 100k sales opportunity exists for customers to take product early.

Discuss and challenge if increased sales people would produce more sales.

Make sure the on-time delivery (otd) targets are real and production signed up to them.

Is the late order catch up the reason for backlog reduction?

Always discuss pricing and how much of any sales forecast change is price v. volume.

DEALING WITH POOR CUSTOMERS

A REAL LIFE EXAMPLE

> **Pay attention. This page can make you a lot of money.**

One way is to list customers into 4 groups:
Good
Could Be Good
Acceptable
X — A Nuisance

A business had 10 X customers that only contributed approximately 5% profit. The sales manager was told to DOUBLE THE PRICES for these customers.

A month later, doubling the prices was not done. Sales folks normally do not like this sort of work.

Two months later, it was still not done.

So the question is WHY? Answer — we will lose the customers.

OK, so how many will you lose? Answer — It could be at least half of them.

Out comes the calculator... Let's assume we lose 6 of the 10. OK?

The sales guy said OK, but he did not expect it to be 6.

Did following sum.

> Current profit from 10 customers at 5% on say sales per customer of 100 ($ or ?) equals 50 (5% on 1000).
>
> Double price for 4 remaining customers profit is 105 per customer equals 420.
>
> Outcome Profit goes from 50 to 420 on sales of 800 (4 x 200 new price) as against profit of 50 on sales of 1000 from 10 customers.

**NET RESULT
SALES FALL FROM 1000 TO 800
PROFIT INCREASES FROM 50 TO 420**

**HAVE DONE THIS SO MANY TIMES AND IT WORKS
BUT ONLY IN THE MARGINS ON A SMALL NUMBER
OF X CUSTOMERS**

THINGS TO LOOK OUT FOR

*This page can make you a lot of money or save you a lot of money.
Full of surprises when you ask!*

Make sure the sales negotiators are financially numerate.

Some questions to ask

- If you mark the cost of a product up by 10% then give the customer a 10% discount, what is the % profit?
- If you mark the cost of a product up by 50%, what is the % Gross Margin?
- If the company bottom line profit is 10% of total sales revenue:

  What will the new profit % be if you give a 5% discount across the board?

  What will the percentage increase in profit be if you increase all prices by 1%?
- If you have a business with a large number of products with a price list, go through the list and selectively price taking a lesson from the grocery business.

  Use price points. Price the most noticeable items competitively. Load less visible items.
- Do an exercise with the sales team. List all of the things you do for customers FREE. See if any of these can be charged for.

Great area for instant 100% profit and cash.

Make sure the SALES TEAM understands the following terms for your business / products / contracts.

PROFIT / GROSS MARGIN / CONTRIBUTION / MARK UP / ABSORBED COST / DIRECT COST

MORE CAN BE LESS

Most businesses chase and maximize sales.
Sometimes taking out the few worst performing lowest margin customers can increase profitability and make the business much more effective.
Less work, more profit.

MEASUREMENT & CONTROLS
If it can not be measured, it can not be managed!

WHY MEASURE?
Provide information
Communication aide
Track specific activities
Identify correct problems early
Determine and justify decisions
Planning aide
Risk management aide

> "In the land of the blind, the one-eyed man is king."
> ~Erasmus

WHY HAVE CONTROLS

AN OPPORTUNITY TO HELP
This provides the senior Executive to take an overview of a situation and see if any help can be provided.

TO INFORM
It provides the information to let Executives know what is going on.

TO POLICE
Make sure company assets are prudently managed and deployed.

KEY POINT
When a control is introduced, Executives often think they are a waste of time as they end up approving everything they see.
The point with a control is that the effectiveness is often invisible as the higher the level of authority, it acts as a deterrent to stop frivolous / marginal requests being presented. Stopped at the source!

You are controlling what you do not see!

KEY PERFORMANCE INDICATORS

KPIs are powerful weapons to improve performance with the following advantages.

The presence of information usually improves performance.
People respond and want to do better if they KNOW what is happening.
A KPI can be introduced quickly from local information.
A KPI can be based on non-financial data.

MOST IMPORTANT

You can often ask the person responsible for the performance to produce the KPI information, thus achieving personal commitment and immediacy of information.

VERY POWERFUL

SALES / PRICING

- Sales / customer
- Margin / customer
- Sales / person
- Sales / customer
- Margin / customer
- Average order size (money or qty.)
- No. of orders / day
- Orders % of tenders (quotes)
- No. of outstanding tenders (quotes)
- Average time to respond to tender (quote)
- New customers / day (week?)
- No. of customer complaints / week
- No. credit notes / week
- Average value credit note
- Average orders / sales person
- Selling cost % / sales
- Market share %
- Debtor (receivables) in days
- Returns by value % of sales
- Sales by product
- Margin % by product
- Sales by territory
- Margin by territory
- Customer quality stats about you
- Average cost / sales person
- Average bonus / sales person
- Bonus (commission) as % sales
- Marketing costs / % sales
- Total selling costs / % sales
- Number of days to prepare a tender (quote)

NUMBERS YOU SHOULD KNOW

TYPICAL COMPANY NUMBERS AS A % OF SALES
On a direct cash basis not absorbed rates

SPEND ON DIRECT MATERIALS	30%
COST OF EMPLOYING PEOPLE	30%
OVERHEADS NON PEOPLE COSTS	30%
PROFIT BEFORE TAX & INTEREST	10%

SOME WHAT IFs?   IMPACT ON PROFIT

UPSIDES

10% INCREASE IN SALES   PROFIT INCREASES BY 40%
With no overhead increase, just direct cost.

5% REDUCTION IN PEOPLE   PROFIT INCREASES BY 15%

5% SAVING IN MATERIAL SPEND PROFIT INCREASES BY 15%

1% INCREASE IN PRICES   PROFIT INCREASES BY 10%

DOWNSIDES

5% INCREASE IN PAY   PROFIT DOWN BY 15%

5% DISCOUNT TO CUSTOMERS   PROFIT DOWN BY 50%

MAKE SURE YOU KNOW THE REAL NUMBERS FOR YOUR BUSINESS

INFORMATION THAT YOU SHOULD KNOW

ALL THE NUMBERS ON PAGE 66 FOR YOUR BUSINESS

IF USING ABSORPTION COSTING, WHAT ARE THE RATES?

What are the actual rates?

How are they costed?

What is the average contribution in the standard rates?

What finance are reporting for over / under absorption (actual numbers)?

WHAT ARE THE FINANCE TEAM POLICIES?

Standard depreciation rates.

Provisioning policy / who makes the decisions and why?

Any cash received sitting in books not matched to a P.O.

What is in obsolete inventory written off? Do you agree?

What are the auditors saying? Ask them before they ask you.

What are they provisioning for problems / warranty returns etc.?

OFF BALANCE SHEET LIABILITIES

Not every financial risk / commitment is in the accounts. Look for some.

Major contract spend.

Cost to complete on major contracts / projects.

Credit / returns / warranty liabilities not fully provisioned.

WHAT COULD GET YOU. STAY IN FRONT OF A POSSIBLE PROBLEM

Foreign exchange volatility.

International changes to commercial policy.

Taxation surprises.

Bank covenants not met.

Legislation / regulation changes.

Inventory write-off.

QUESTIONS TO ASK

AND KNOW THE ANSWERS

> **THE MORE YOU KNOW, THE MORE YOU REALIZE WHAT YOU DO NOT KNOW**

> **JUDGE A PERSON BY THEIR QUESTIONS NOT THEIR ANSWERS**

WHO? WHAT? WHERE? WHEN? HOW? WHY?

ALWAYS GOOD START

ROLL OF QUESTIONS

One of the definitions of an effective Executive that I like is:

"The ability to learn on your feet without appearing to do so."

General Managers usually do not know about every function that they may be responsible for. One of the ways to improve your knowledge is to ask questions. This section is intended to act as a guide to this process.

Most of these questions are closed with numerate answers required.

To discover more about the Executive, use OPEN questions.

> **DO LISTEN TO THE ANSWERS REALLY LISTEN**

> *"A fool can ask a question that a thousand wise men cannot answer."*
> ~G. Torriano

QUESTIONS TO ASK

This whole book has hopefully got across that QUESTIONS lead to ANSWERS.

**Maybe not the ones you would like.
But at least you know! Maybe?**

SOME RANDOM QUESTIONS TO ASK THE FINANCE DEPARTMENT

CASH AT BANK?

Review latest numbers?

What costing system in use?

Any pending write-offs / obsolescence due? Ask for audit management letter.

Relationship with auditors?

IT platform?

Financial timetable for year / Budget Variance analysis discussion to budget.

What control systems does the finance team operate? Maybe independently?

Is there anything you want to tell me? Always interesting!

Do you have any ideas to improve the business?

What wastes most of your time?

How do you rate my performance?

Review all major prepayments and accruals. See if you agree.

TIME / ACCURACY / COST

IDEAL WORLD

Perfect accurate information on time.

REAL WORLD

Imperfect information that takes time and can be expensive to produce.

ISSUES and CONSIDERATIONS

Review what is required / when / level of accuracy. Be precise.

Check if the finance department are overloaded. Set priorities.

Try and use standard data readily available.

ACTIVITIES THAT COST A LOT OF MONEY

> The next few pages are about some typical activities that are a part of business life. They do how however have some high cost implications and some of these issues have been detailed.

ACTIVITIES THAT COST A LOT OF MONEY

PICKING A FIGHT

Very rarely do we have to fight to protect the integrity of the business. Usually we fight for all sorts of other reasons often to do with bad communications and egos, there are always two sides to most stories, and if you involve lawyers many more sides to all stories. Before you start down this road and spend almost certainly a lot of money, commit a lot of time and probably drain your emotional energy.
Ask a few basic questions.

Do I have to as a matter of fundamental integrity?

How much money will it cost?

Do they owe us money? (You should get this back first.)

How much time will it take?

What are the chances of winning? (An outright victory is very rare.)

What emotional cost will it take?

Look at the answers and take a financially based decision!

If important ask an objective outside executive (not lawyer) for an opinion

HIRING CONSULTANTS

Can be very effective, but usually they are not. So many times I have seen consultants come in, talk to your people wrap it all up in a nice report and feed it back to top management. So get out and walk about (MBWA) and find out what's going on in your business before you reach for a consultant. Having got that out the way! Consultants can be of great use in two situations. Firstly, if they have a very focused and specific area of knowledge and expertise that the business does not have or secondly, where you do not have enough resources and a temporary (interim) solution may be cost effective. Make sure that you do not get the two mixed up as the highly focused specialist will probably be very expensive and you do not want that higher cost rate applied to interim and possible routine executive work. Pay for the expertise, not all the leg work that goes with it. Consultants have a mission to upsell this to clients.

ACTIVITIES THAT COST A LOT OF MONEY

BUYING ANOTHER BUSINESS / ACQUISITIONS

Buying another business can be exciting, game changing and a great strategic move. You have approximately a 50% probability of that being true. In all cases it will cost you a lot of money and time, and the integration is never as easy as it may at first appear. Cultural misalignment being a major reason why acquisitions do not work. Be objective, realistic and do not fall in love with the idea. Listen to the finance team. They normally provide the "why it is not a good idea" view with a dose of healthy cynicism as they normally have to do most of the work and sort out the failures.

RECRUITMENT

Recruitment can be essential in times of growth or normal replacements and can be effective to revitalize a business by bringing in new people with different experiences and energy levels. Just be aware that it is expensive not only the fees paid, but in the time to induct new people and the consequent disruption to the business. The very best recruitment outcomes are usually only 50 to 60% effective. Please avoid the temptation to be macho man and go around firing everyone. You are paid to manage the company resources effectively That includes the people who you may inherit in your team, firing has to be a last resort and only when all your management skills have been exhausted and you have given up. (Note this 1st point is more about you getting performance out of them than them doing it for you. Both are required, of course.)

OPENING UP ANOTHER SITE

Sometimes essential for expansion, but multiple sites often dramatically increase costs and make communications worse, especially if a long distance or another country is involved. Make sure you have really run the actual numbers. Then double them and see it still works. If not, the move is so marginal that it is not worth the risk. Wherever possible max out the space utilization on existing footprints, pack them in and get great cost utilization. Look at outsourcing as an alternative.

ACTIVITIES THAT COST A LOT OF MONEY

DEALING WITH BANKS

The basic point to always remember is that a **BANK IS A BUSINESS** and it has to make money, and guess where that money is coming from? Banks are of course a fundamental part of life in that their central role is to take money from people who do not need it and lend it to people that do, charging interest which they split up between themselves, the original lender and the tax man. Modern banking however is much more complex than this and a whole range of special products have been invented by the bank to achieve their central aim of making more money. Pay attention to the small print. Especially change and transaction fees, as this is where they can make a lot of money. Banks and other professional bodies like change because they deal in change and receive fees mainly for managing change. Acquisitions, refinancing, new loans, etc. A few tips for dealing with the banks.

Maintain good relationships, especially during good times. It may help at a bad time.

Talk to them immediately about a problem. They like surprises less than you do.

Note that valuations change if in distress. Inventory / Debtors / Assets marked down.

Try and deal in numbers, not percentages. Especially on large transaction fees.

Ask for advice. They know a lot of stuff and people.

Expect totally rational economic behavior. They have tight regulations.

They will try and get you to do transactions. They make money off the change not the outcome, so make sure that the anticipated result is in your best long-term interest.

Avoid covenant breaches, fees will be high. Anticipate this when you agree to them.

Try to ensure your lead bank limits the amount of debt syndication (the number of other banks that they involve in the debt schedule). More fees.

ACTIVITIES THAT COST A LOT OF MONEY

MAJOR PROJECTS AND CONTRACTS

For some businesses this will be their main activity carrying out large contract work for customers. For nearly all businesses, once in a while a major contract or project comes along that has to be managed. So this page illustrates some of the key issues that have to be taken into account on large contract accounting.

ESTIMATING is fundamentally important and should be realistic and checked by an expert.

Appoint a competent **FINANCIALLY literate** project manager.

Review costs on a regular and ongoing basis

Do a regular **COST TO COMPLETE REVIEW**. Do not wait until job is finished.

Have strict **CONTROLS FOR VARIATIONS / ADDITIONS,** etc. You to sign?

Develop a contingency **RISK MITIGATION** plan

For commercial work, charge the customer for variations in small amounts on a regular basis. Do not wait until the end of the contract for a large sum which will inevitability be negotiated down.

Understand the ebb and flow of power and the buyer's risk during the length of the contract. Job finished and a dispute with you not having been paid? Tricky?

INSURE for risk where you are able to.

Make sure the contract is **FULLY CLOSED** and signed off with any retentions collected.

Watch the **CASH FLOWS,** especially on international work.

ACTIVITIES THAT COST A LOT OF MONEY

THE CALL FROM OVERSEAS

I put this in for amusement, but with serious message. It used to be quite common for the GM or CFO to receive a call from an alleged prince or government official from a foreign country that has millions in a bank and unfortunately is unable to get them out of the country. If only you could help by providing details of your bank account he would be pleased to split the proceeds with you. Clearly a scam, which would have resulted in an empty bank account. Interestingly I have heard that some people actually fell for this. Amazing. The point is that if it sounds too good to be true then it usually is.
Some other calls that may cost you money.

You or your business are wonderful and have been chosen.

To feature in an article in our magazine

>Providing you buy advertising or give us a list of your customers / suppliers so we can hit them for advertising.

To make a movie

>Providing you meet the $XXX production costs and we have plans to show this on the next overnight flight to Mongolia in a year's time. Not that there is anything wrong with Mongolia, some of my best friends come from there.

To speak at our next major conference

>We expect all your customers to attend, especially once we have signed you up, and guess what the registration fee is for you and your company — only $XXX.

To invest in this exciting new opportunity

>Early groundbreaking, innovative opportunity. Have your credit card ready. What was the business again?

*Some of these are of course legitimate businesses,
but they do not usually cold call.*

ACTIVITIES THAT COST A LOT OF MONEY

FAILING TO MANAGE PEOPLE

This is a reminder that although this book focuses on numeracy and the more hard nosed aspects of a business the leading, motivation and management of people is fundamental to success. A team that is engaged and feels part of the organization and that feels that their contribution is respected and recognized performs better. In my experience some of the more heroic work with regard to long arduous hours on not too inspiring work is often done by the finance team. It is the nature of the job to produce a lot of data that must hit deadlines. A disengaged team will be less productive and will also often have more absence and a higher turnover of staff. All of which cost a lot of money. **Some simple things you can do to lead and inspire.**

Walk about ask questions and **LISTEN,** really listen.

Show interest in what people are doing.

Say thank you once in a while.

Recognize a good performance, maybe a small incentive. Buy a pizza for the team.

Become involved in training programs and plans.

Hold a town hall meeting in the Finance Department once in a while. Tell them what is going on in the business.

Recognize periods of hard work. For example, month end / year end closing books.

Ask for advice / comments. Finance people see a lot and from an interesting perspective.

Make sure priorities and expectations (your's and their's) are set correctly.

Show interest, listen, recognize contribution and say thank you…..It's not hard!

NOTE: This section applies to the whole company, not just the finance team.

ACTIVITIES THAT COST A LOT OF MONEY

GOING INTERNATIONAL
A great way to expand a business is through international sales. It enables you to address new markets, create dedicated products and services and you get to travel and see the world. Always an educational pleasure. However it has some situations that you have to be aware of.

Make sure that the CASH FLOWS and PAYMENT TERMS work.

Fully understand the FCPA (Foreign and Corrupt Practices Act if in USA).

Beware hidden costs. Travel / Agents / Duties / Customs / Local tariffs, taxes, etc. MANY!

Check your TRANSFER PRICING assumptions with Auditors. Tax authorities have to agree.

Take into account language and cultural factors.

Make sure time zone differences not an issue.

Understand the supply chain / distribution channel of the country where you are operating.

Calculate risk of failure / obsolescence.

Look for any distribution channel conflict. Agents handling competitors products.

Check if financial help available from your government. Trade shows missions.

Check if financial help available in the target country. Grants / Tax breaks.

Do not underestimate in-house support costs. Language skills.

Seek and use local help.

Note that jet lag effect / tiredness can affect judgment.

Communication costs can be high. Check out cell phone tariffs before travel.

AGAIN...Make sure that the CASH FLOWS and PAYMENT TERMS work.

ACTIVITIES THAT COST A LOT OF MONEY

LAWYERS

I will resist all the jokes and other comments and stay on the high ground. This profession is an essential part of the business world to the extent that I have seen some reports that it costs American business circa 5% of corporate revenues. Seems high, but if you take into account all the ancillary and related other similar professional services it could be high enough to warrant some financial control, which is after all why it is in this section. Some basic points to bear in mind when dealing with the legal profession from a financial control perspective.

Decide if you require to employ an in-house attorney. Outside services will probably always be required, but an in-house service could reduce the TOTAL cost of legal services.

Lawyers work by the hour and typically charge in 15 minute segments on an absorbed cost rate, which can be several hundred dollars per hour.

If you waste the time of a lawyer, unlike you, this is probably good news for them as they get to charge you more.

Just because they are usually very smart, please recognize that they work for a business with the same objectives as you. To make as much money as possible.

Law firms carry out the same sales techniques as any other business and you should recognize them.

UPSELLING — Extending time and brief, involving other lawyers.

CROSS SELLING — Providing other services, maybe of an admin nature that you could do in-house cheaper.

Hire a good and busy lawyer, if possible. Maybe a higher rate per hour, but they have reduced incentive / opportunity to take longer. Maybe cheaper in long run.

Law firms usually expect the time charge to be negotiated at the end of a long contract. The hours often resulting in an over absorbed profit, which many firms will trade down if asked. Do not disappoint them!

Try and obtain a fixed quote and price for the work, which the lawyer will stick to. Please let me know if you manage to do this.

Check out conflicts of interest before starting any work. This will avoid maybe having to abort a job.

Before picking a fight, read page 72. Only guaranteed winners are the lawyers, usually paid win or lose.

BUSINESS REVIEW PROCESS

> It is a an important part of the executive process to check the budget / plan to see what is actually happening. Someone will be checking up on you. You should be checking up on your team and you should be checking up on yourself. These two pages explain an EXECUTIVE REVIEW PROCESS that I have been using for a long time, and before writing this section I quickly calculated that I must have carried out at least 2500 review meetings using this format. The majority from the position of Group CEO reviewing operating stand-alone profit subsidiaries, usually in person and if not, then by phone. The objective is to do this review every month. I know it works and is very effective providing you follow the rules below and stick to the agenda opposite.

MEETING RULES

Start the meeting by explaining the following:
This is a review of the EXECUTIVE process and top level business performance
"It is not a detailed talking meeting about how to do things."
It is to check that things that are required to be done are identified and are being done. Everyone should take the perspective of a business reviewer taking the helicopter view.

Heads of functions only. Ideally less than 10 people.

Agenda fixed as opposite.

Short, sharp and punchy.

Open discussion. All present to discuss any subject.

Direct open language. No after the meeting chats with me. Even if it means criticizing the GM in an open meeting.

Healthy debate is good. The GM should encourage active criticism if well intended.

No grudges, no retributions, just tell it how it is and deal with it.

BUSINESS REVIEW MEETING AGENDA

1. **MINUTES** Check everyone has a set of current action minutes (see below).

2. **TRADING / MAJOR ISSUES OVERVIEW.** This sets the tone for the meeting and important issues (like a cash crisis) should not have to wait for an agenda item. Check performance to budget / plan. Discuss environment briefly. Unless issues.

3. **ORDERS / SALES.** Market? Sales performance, customers, competitors activity, sales team morale?

4. **OPERATIONS.** Quick look at top level efficiency reports. Any issues?

5. **QUALITY.** Look at statistics / On-time delivery / Customer service / Complaints?

6. **CASH**. Any issues, any ideas to create more, any large items of expenditure on way?

7. **CAPITAL EXPENDITURE.** Any approvals required?

8. **PEOPLE**. Any issues at all? Not just the HR report!

9. **LEGAL**. Anyone suing us or is anyone being sued by us? FCPA any issues.

10. **FORECAST** Short-term next 4 weeks, plus general outlook / issues? Agree the immediate business targets.

11. **NEXT MEETING DATE** (usually 4 weeks time).

ACTION MINUTES. These are based on each meeting having a number and the actions at the meetings are referenced to the meeting number. So at meeting 1, all the agreed actions will 1.1, 1.2, 1.3, etc. At meeting 2, if any of the actions 1 have been completed, then they are deleted. Actions arising at meeting 2 are designated 2.1, 2.2, etc. The benefit of this approach is that there are no long-winded minutes just actions cleared and if you are at meeting 10 and there is still a 1.7 on minutes that says 10 months still not done. Pressure.

FRAUD & DISHONESTY

A PERSPECTIVE

In my early career I did a lot of work on fraud prevention and detection working for a major brewing company that had several pubs with lots of cash and a presence of alcohol. You can imagine the opportunities for wrongdoing were many and various and we of course, had to deal with all the unsuccessful criminals and thieves. The successful ones got away undetected and there must have been some. This work resulted in dealing with the police fraud squads and inevitably exchanging experiences. An interesting perspective from them was that they had two major observations. Detection was usually as a result of some other unfortunate circumstance, bad luck if you will, and not the routine audit. Secondly, that the number one suspect was the superficially loyal employee that had been there years, never took a vacation, always first in and last to leave, worked long hours and knew everything about the business. It is a bit like the most likely person to murder you is your significant other, so that's where the police start, the innocent partners that are genuinely grieved at their loss have to face becoming the number one suspect. You cannot blame the police. They are just working the numbers. I am not suggesting that you suspect the vast majority of hard working people in your company that fit this profile of fraud. Just be aware that fraud and wrongdoing can pop up anywhere and it can result in serious problems. A balanced perspective between trust and awareness is required by the GM. Do not rely on the finance and audit teams to uncover problems.

TIPS FOR THE GM TO HELP PREVENT FRAUD

For key high-risk positions:

    Rotate staff, if possible.

    Ensure that they take a vacation / training away. Job breaks of at least 2 weeks.

Check and sign the payroll personally.

Look at the bank statements / query anything you do not understand.

Spot check expense reports / invoices without a purchase order.

Look at company payments schedule see if any companies that you do not recognize.

> "The creation of phantom companies is an old one."

Talk to the external auditors and ask if they have any concerns.

Spot check factory completion notes to ensure that the product has been invoiced.

Check if any employees appear to have a lifestyle well above their income. Investigate if suspicious.

Check all competitive tendering process see if they are fair.

Ask accountants if any money has been received with no Purchase Order or invoice. It happens!

Institute criminal record checks if key job.

You will almost certainly not come across any fraudulent behavior doing these things, you will however probably find a few interesting surprises. The point is that if people know that you are aware and checking up on things, this will act as a deterrent. As with many controls, you are controlling what you do not see.

DEALING WITH ACCOUNTANTS

Most accountants are pretty smart and well-trained by their profession, have access to a lot of critical information and usually find out things about the financial structure of a business before other management. Plus, they usually have a responsibility to meet fiscal standards, laws, audit best practice, etc. that may in some instances create a higher level of responsibility than that to the GM they may report to. This awesome series of attributes provides them with a major power base. They also usually have access to outside bodies like banks where there opinions are encouraged and they may be asked what they think of the management. You?

This set of attributes may result in them being intimidating and difficult to deal with, especially as they speak their own language. When I trained as a Mechanical Engineer and then worked as a systems analyst I developed many of the schematics and material in this book to explain the concepts of financial control to non-financial managers. I know that they work well and have stood the test of time.

The relationship between the GM / CEO and the CFO is the most important senior management relationship in any business and that it is fundamental to the good management and governance of any business. When the chips are down it is usually just those two executives sitting in a room trying to figure out what to do? So work at this relationship. A very competent finance executive with whom you have a good relationship is fundamental, plus they will look out for you.

The other key point to make about the finance function is that a set of accounts includes many judgments and estimates often made by the finance team. The accounts are usually presented with good clarity and certainty and for sure most of the numbers will have been checked, cross referenced, balanced etc., but then someone will have to make a judgment call on certain issues. You need to make sure that you know what these areas are in the accounts and that you agree with them.

Finally this book uses simple terms and accountants can use different words, but they all at some point have to get back to the basic terms used in this book.

TOP TIPS FOR FINANCIAL WELL-BEING

1. TAKE THE BUSINESS PERFORMANCE PERSONAL AND FEEL ACCOUNTABLE
2. FOCUS ON CASH
3. GET INVOLVED IN PRICING DECISIONS
4. UNDERSTAND THE ABSORPTION COSTING SYSTEM. CONTRIBUTION!
5. FORM A GOOD RELATIONSHIP WITH THE CFO / FD
6. UNDERSTAND PROFIT V. CASH AND THEIR INTER-RELATIONSHIP
7. MAKE SURE SALES / ESTIMATING TEAM ARE FINANCIALLY LITERATE
8. STAY CLOSE TO THE AUDITORS
9. BEWARE OF HOCKEY STICK FORECASTS. ALL COMING GOOD IN LAST Q
10. TALK TO THE BANKS EVEN WHEN THINGS ARE GOING WELL
11. ASK QUESTIONS. ALWAYS ASK QUESTIONS
12. UNDERSTAND WHAT JUDGMENT DECISIONS THE FINANCE TEAM ARE MAKING
13. KEEP THE BOARD UP TO SPEED
14. FOCUS ON PRIORITIES. PARETO ANALYSIS 80:20 RULE
15. MAKE SURE INCENTIVE SCHEMES TARGET YOUR OBJECTIVES
16. STAY COOL IN A CRISIS

BE NICE TO PEOPLE. THEY WILL HELP YOU AND TELL YOU THINGS?
NB. FAIR AND DEMANDING BUT NICE

BASIC ACCOUNTING TERMS EXPLAINED

DOUBLE ENTRY / DEBITS / CREDITS / T ACCOUNTS

DOUBLE ENTRY CONCEPT

To close a set of accounts the BALANCE SHEET has to BALANCE. The way this is best done on a transactional basis is that every transaction when it is entered into the BOOKS OF ACCOUNT (or LEDGERS) has two entries one for each side of the BALANCE SHEET. The accountants use several different accounts to do this so that when the are all added up they will balance. This is called the DOUBLE ENTRY SYSTEM. The earliest examples of this system allegedly being credited to Luca Pacioli in the 15th Century.

DEBITS / CREDITS / T ACCOUNTS

Debits and credits form two opposite aspects of every financial transaction. In basic terms, debit simply means left side, and credit means right side. The BALANCE SHEET has two sides. One side is Assets and the other side is Liabilities and EQUITY (Owners P&L). Just to confuse everyone some liabilities are shown as Negative Assets and are shown on the left hand side of the balance sheet as negative. For example, you will see on page 15 that the CREDITORS are NETTED of DEBTORS as against being shown on the right hand side of the Balance Sheet as a Liability. An increase (+) to an asset account is a debit. An increase (+) to a liability account is a credit. Conversely, a decrease (-) to an asset account is a credit. A decrease (-) to a liability account is a debit.

EXAMPLES

On the page opposite is a very simple work through from the Double entries of the PRIME TRANSACTION through to a P&L Account and then into a BALANCE SHEET. Note the T in the accounts. The use of the DEBIT or CREDIT and which side of the T account that it goes will depend upon what type of account that it is. Asset, Liability, Income. Expense or Equity / Capital. Below are the way DEBIT or CREDIT is applied.

- **A** ASSET account. Increase is a DEBIT and decrease is a CREDIT (To BS)
- **L** LIABILITY account. Increase is a CREDIT and decrease is a DEBIT (To BS)
- **I** INCOME account. Increase is a CREDIT and decrease is a DEBIT (To P&L)
- **E** EXPENSE account. Increase is a DEBIT and decrease is a CREDIT (To P&L)
- **C** CAPITAL/ EQUITY account. Increase is a DEBIT and decrease is a CREDIT (To BS)

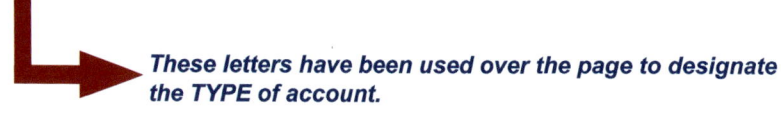

These letters have been used over the page to designate the TYPE of account.

BASIC ACCOUNTING
EXAMPLES

	PRIME ENTRIES DOUBLE ENTRY TRANSACTION	ACCOUNT NAME	ACC TYPE	DEBIT	CREDIT	
1	Borrow $2000 from Bank	LOAN	L		2000	
		CASH	A	2000		
2	Raw material purchased for CASH $200	CASH	A		200	
		INVENTORY	A	200		12
3	Stock count produces $40 write off	INVENTORY	A		40	
		STOCK WRITE OFF	E	40		SEPARATE
4	Weekly payroll $50 CASH	CASH	A		50	EVENTS
		LABOR	E	50		
5	Material used in production and sold $180	INVENTORY	A		180	
		COST OF SALES	E	180		
6	Sales of $100 paid CASH	SALES	I		100	
		CASH	A	100		
7	Sales $400 on credit	SALES	I		400	12
		PAYABLES	A	400		SEPARATE
8	Customer pays $50 due DEBT	CASH	A	50		EVENTS
		PAYABLES	A		50	
9	Raw material purhased for credit $400	INVENTORY	A	400		
		CREDITORS	L		400	
10	Pay Supplier $100	CASH	A		100	
		CREDITOR	L	100		
11	Pay all overheads CASH $120	OVERHEADS	I	120		
		CASH	A		120	
12	Bank interest paid. $20	INTEREST PAID	E	20		
		CASH	A		20	
		BALANCE		3660	3660	

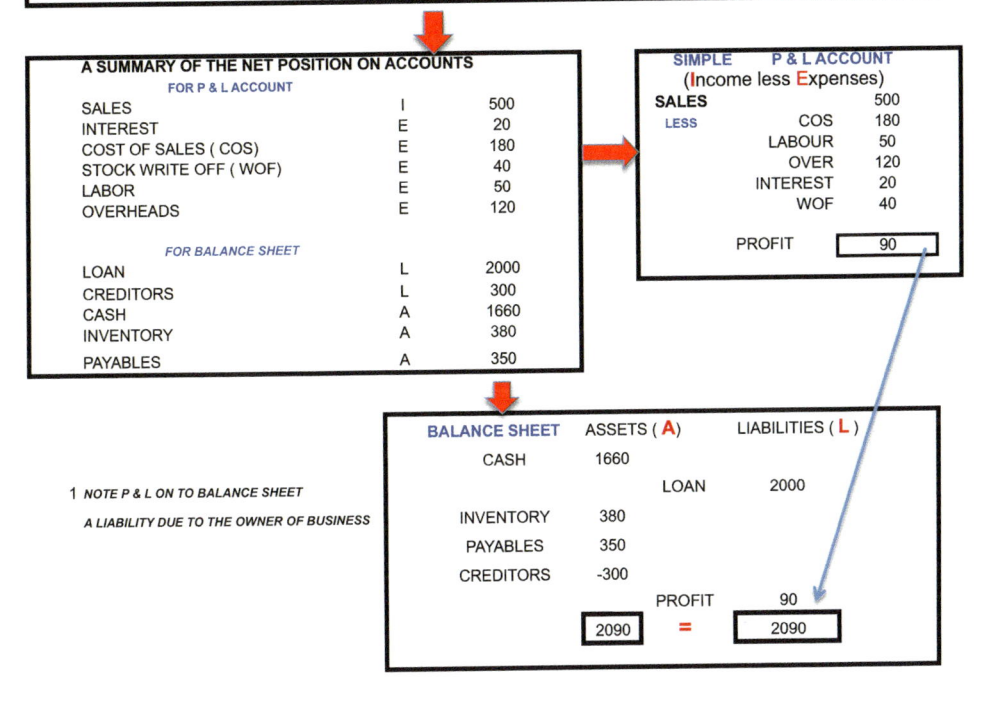

A SUMMARY OF THE NET POSITION ON ACCOUNTS

FOR P & L ACCOUNT

SALES	I	500
INTEREST	E	20
COST OF SALES (COS)	E	180
STOCK WRITE OFF (WOF)	E	40
LABOR	E	50
OVERHEADS	E	120

FOR BALANCE SHEET

LOAN	L	2000
CREDITORS	L	300
CASH	A	1660
INVENTORY	A	380
PAYABLES	A	350

SIMPLE P & L ACCOUNT
(**I**ncome less **E**xpenses)

SALES			500
LESS		COS	180
		LABOUR	50
		OVER	120
		INTEREST	20
		WOF	40
		PROFIT	90

1 NOTE P & L ON TO BALANCE SHEET
A LIABILITY DUE TO THE OWNER OF BUSINESS

BALANCE SHEET

	ASSETS (**A**)	LIABILITIES (**L**)
CASH	1660	
LOAN		2000
INVENTORY	380	
PAYABLES	350	
CREDITORS	-300	
PROFIT		90
	2090 =	2090

A DAY WITH A CEO — FINANCE   COPYRIGHT BRIAN MOORE   PAGE 87

VALUING A BUSINESS

VALUING A BUSINESS

The actual value for any BUSINESS is the price on the contract when a transaction has been completed. To help in the process of reaching that valuation several methods may be used and they are briefly discussed below. A discerning buyer will value the business probably using most of these methods before deciding what the business is worth to them.

PUBLICLY QUOTED COMPANY

The starting point will always be the MARKET CAPITALIZATION of the business. Number of shares times current price. Strict rules apply as to how to conduct any offers or express interest in acquiring a quoted company but as a general rule the BOARD would only consider any offers at a premium to the shares price. We could dedicate many words to the process requirements that follows an offer of interest but the key factor is if the TARGET company being approached is amenable to a deal or is it hostile. Valuations below could still apply, but they are usually for PRIVATE COMPANIES.

ASSET VALUATION

From the balance sheet see what the NET Assets are supporting the value. Then take a view what those assets are worth to you. This will require in "DUE DILIGENCE," checking areas like inventory and payables to see if they are GOOD. Some of the assets can be widely under or over valued, a point you should always be aware. A short while back some CORPORATE RAIDERS made a lot of money by acquiring companies that had dramatically undervalued assets, mainly land. For example, the struggling engineering company in a downtown location with the land value not reflected in the balance sheet at value. Someone buys the company cheap, closes it or even sells trading business to someone else, then flattens the site and sells for a fortune or maybe puts a shopping mall up. Be vigilant about balance sheet valuations.

PROFIT MULTIPLE

This is the more normal valuation for a good business that typically has good prospects of growth. The normal multiple is of EBITDA (Earnings Before Interest Tax and Depreciation). The benefit of this approach is that it can be used as a comparison to other companies regardless of size (Asset value). Areas to watch are which EBITDA valuation to use, TRAILING for the buyer, or projected for the seller can be a huge difference. This should be compared to the SALES MULTIPLE.

EXPECTATION, HOPE, MASSIVE GAMBLE or BUSINESS JUDGEMENT?

This normally applies to a high tech company in an early stage of its life. Your hope is that you are acquiring a "Google" or a "Facebook," but the reality is that most of these companies crash and burn into oblivion very early and take all the investments down. Some of the valuations for these companies are interesting maybe many times sales multiple for a company that maybe has yet to make a profit?

BRINGING IT TOGETHER

Before proceeding with any serious attempts to acquire a business then all valuation methods should be used and compared to risk. For example, you may accept that an EBITDA multiple of 10 times was OK, but the Assets valuation maybe revealed twice the balance sheet value and maybe 5 times sales revenue. May still be a good idea, but the risk profile is increasing.

ANALYTICAL TECHNIQUES & ACCOUNTING TOOLS

THE USE OF ANALYTICAL TOOLS

The most effective analytical tool in my experience is to ask **WHY?** But as this is not very scientific, this section is intended to make you aware of some of the other techniques and tools that are available. Just in case you needed some more academic help.

ZERO BASED BUDGETING (Zero sum)

This is so simple that I am always amazed that it actually has the life it does. Either you take last years' budget, look at any significant variances and prepare the next year's budget, or you start with a ZERO BASE and build all the numbers up from a clean sheet (i.e,. ZERO BASED BUDGETING).

ACTIVITY SAMPLING

A statistical technique where by if you take random observations of an event that will enable you to extrapolate the full-time meaning of that activity within certain tolerance or level of accuracy. For example, if you look out the window and see that someone is at the coffee store 25 times out of 50 observations you could work out that the store is busy between say 45 to 55% of the time. Depending upon the number of observations and the total time over which they are taken. This saves your time as you do not have to watch the coffee store 100% of the time if the answer to within + /- 5% is acceptable.
Trade of time versus accuracy.

FINANCIAL MODELING

Financial modeling is usually carried out by people outside the business by organizations that have an interest in its performance. Especially if you are a public company then many investment analysts, banks, private equity shops and others will be developing financial models for your business. The analysts preparing the model will of course mainly be using data in the public domain. They will try to get access to management to obtain information that will enable them to develop a more realistic model. This can be dangerous, especially for managers in a public company. There are rules! The internal version of modeling is more typically described as budgeting or financial planning.

ANALYTICAL TECHNIQUES & ACCOUNTING TOOLS

DISCOUNTED CASH FLOW or IRR (Internal Rate of Return)

A technique for taking all future CASH (only cash) projections back to the present day value taking into account the cost of money over the life of the project. For example, inflation indices, cost, wage drift, etc. This is usually used as an investment appraisal tool. A simple example. You invest $100 today and you will receive $150 back in 10 years. The value of $50 in 10 years in today's CASH would probably be guess? Say $25. So the investment return in Net Present Day terms using Discounted Cash Flow (DCF) is 25% not the headline 50%. The financial services industry and credit card companies use these concepts to great effect as a sales tool to provide an illusion of higher than real returns or costs. This is why they have to put numbers in like the equivalent APR. My old boss used to dismiss any DCF supported investment proposal out of hand as he considered that if it required a DCF analysis to support the idea, then it was so marginal as to not warrant his consideration.
Bit over the to,p but he had a point.

PAYROLL DRIFT ANALYSIS

This is one of mine. Mainly designed to achieve a look of consternation on the face of an accountant when I ask them what their "Payroll Drift Analysis" shows? Putting that to one side. The serious point is that if you employ a lot of people, they cost a lot of money and that cost requires to be controlled. Payroll Drift is the "cost creep" in employment costs that can be difficult to measure and consequently control. For example, if a business has 100 people each with an average budgeted cost of $50000 each and the agreed pay increase budgeted is 2%, then at the end of the year the actual payroll cost should be $510000 (100 x $50000 + 2%). If that is not the actual income then the difference, which is *usually higher* is termed "Payroll Drift" and requires to be analyzed. Of course the actuals could be lower, which would be negative payroll drift. The prime control measure is a KPI for cost per person. However, other KPIs can be cascaded down from this top level KPI to control any specific activity that is causing the payroll costs to drift away from the PRIME BUDGET ASSUMPTIONS. Areas that cause PAYROLL DRIFT are; Replacing people at a higher cost, doubling up people during hand over / recruitment, additional payments for bonuses / overtime / pay increases, recruiting additional people, giving benefits away, etc.

Negative PAYROLL DRIFT is of course the opposite. For example, running with open vacancies for an extended time. This whole area of PEOPLE COSTS is a potential judgmental conflict for most GMs as on the one hand People costs are usually significant and require to be tightly controlled, yet on the other hand the motivation of people is critical to the success of any business. A question of balance and judgment.

ANALYTICAL TECHNIQUES & ACCOUNTING TOOLS

STATISTICAL SAMPLING

There are many and various techniques for statistical sampling nearly all based around the standard distribution (Bell Curve) and intended to save time by looking at a few carefully chosen sampling techniques. Be aware that they exist and chose your weapon of choice depending upon the circumstances. Always remember accuracy and time cost money, so make sure that you know the levels of accuracy that you are happy to accept. The tighter the tolerance the more expensive it is to find out the information that you require.

VARIANCE ANALYSIS

If you are working to a budget the VARIANCE is the difference between the BUDGET and ACTUAL. Pretty obvious. Variance analysis attempts to provide a more analytical approach to reviewing a variance with the objective of improving the accuracy of forecasting. In my view this is only really effective with a fairly stable business where the statistical tools can be more predictive. Most businesses in my experience produce variances that stand alone and warrant individual assessment. I believe most managers are smart enough to understand instinctively the longer term impact of trending variances.

CRITICAL PATH ANALYSIS

This is a planning technique whereby you identify all the individual dependencies of a major project (maybe list out on a GANTT chart) and then work out the path that drives the length of time the project will take. This enables the focus to be on the critical path items in order to deliver the project on time. A simple example: cooking a meal that requires an oven roast taking 2 hours, plus vegetables and the preparation of the table. The cooking time will drive the total project time so for example, the critical path would be: prepare meat, cook meat, take meat out and serve. The non-critical items that could be done at any time during that critical path, maybe 3 hours, would be prepare and cook vegetables 30 minutes and prepare the table 20 minutes. Simple really, but the component interdependencies and the critical path may not always be obvious unless laid out in a formal way. A point for the GM is that this type of tool is frequently used in a production or engineering environment and maybe not in the finance office. You may want to have a look at see what planning tools the accountants use. You may be able to help.

BREAK EVEN ANALYSIS

Page 24 shows the break even chart for a business and break even analysis would be the way it is calculated. For large projects involving expenditure and income. It is always a good idea to calculate the break even point in numerate and time terms. A good discipline. I have actually witnessed projects that actually never break even when you apply this very simple technique. As I write this page my brain is saying that these things are so simple everyone must get this and do it as a matter of common sense. But then I look back and remember so many times when these obvious things have not been done and common sense is far from common. So if you think this is mind-blowingly simply obvious, then trust me it is not to a lot of people. Quite often in high places!

ANALYTICAL TECHNIQUES & ACCOUNTING TOOLS

RATIO ANALYSIS

A RATIO is created by dividing two or numbers into each other to produce one number. The RATIO can stand alone as fact but more usually for comparison reasons. Compared to either trends within the business.

OR

To compare with other companies to produce a comparative measure (Peer group comp).

A RATIO is a specific type of KPI (Key Performance Indicator).

SOME COMMON RATIOS

LIQUIDITY

QUICK RATIO = CURRENT ASSETS / CURRENT LIABILITIES — **IMPORTANT LOWER THAN 1**

TO TEST BUSINESS ABILITY TO MEET DEBTS

INVENTORY

STOCK TURNS PER YR = SALES / INVENTORY — **CASH IMPLICATIONS**

THE HIGHER THE BETTER

DEBT SERVICE

DEBT EBITDA = DEBT / EBITDA

CONFIDENCE ON ABILITY TO PAY DEBT

RETURN EQUITY

RETURN ON EQUITY = NET INCOME / EQUITY

HOPEFULLY BETTER THAN THE BANK

CASH UTILIZATION

HOW EFFECT CASH USED = CASH / PROFIT — **RECONCILE IF NOT DONE**

SEE PAGE 23

PROFITABILITY

RETURN ON SALES = NET INCOME / NET SALES — **HIGHER BETTER**

TO CHECK RETURN ON SALES

PROFITABILITY

RETURN ON SALES = OPERATING INCOME / NET SALES — **HIGHER BETTER**

TO CHECK RETURN ON SALES

PRODUCTIVITY

SALES PER PERSON = SALES / HEAD COUNT — **GOOD ONE FOR INCENTIVES**

COULD BE MANY OTHER AREAS TO DIVIDE HEAD COUNT INTO

INTEREST COVER

ABILITY TO PAY = CASH / INTEREST

TYPICAL BANK COVENANT

DEBT COVER

TOTAL DEBT / TOTAL EQUITY

CREDITORS INTERESTED IN HOW WELL PROTECTED

MANY MORE RATIOS EXIST OR CAN BE CREATED
MAKE SURE THAT YOU SELECT OR DESIGN THE MOST APPROPRIATE ONES FOR YOUR BUSINESS

ALWAYS CHECK THE BANK COVENANTS MAKE SURE YOU CAN MEET THEM
IDEALLY A RATIO SHOULD RESULT IN THE HIGHER THE NUMBER THE BETTER

ACCOUNTING STANDARDS

PUBLISHED ACCOUNTS

This book focuses on the basic accounting required to run a business. Taking the internal set of accounts to produce another set of accounts that may be published or used by the authorities for example to work out the tax due. This is a whole new area. The difference between the two sets of accounts is mainly due to the professional accountants / auditors applying all of the required ACCOUNTING STANDARDS FOR REPORTING. The essential status and standing of the business remains the same, but the reconciliation between the basic accounts and those reported can be a large and complicated subject. An understanding of the basic treatments of the key areas especially inventory is required. You may receive some nasty shocks when the accountants TELL YOU what has to be reported and how. Sometimes this can be good news. Stay close to the finance team when the published accounts are being prepared.

WHY HAVE STANDARDS?

The main reason is to achieve a standard way of reporting the performance of a company on ideally a universal basis. These standard reports can then be used by the external bodies like the tax authorities, banks, etc. The same terminology and accounting treatments being understood by everyone. Standards are also intended to ensure that the reports are fair and representative, no creative accounting, and hopefully to limit fraud.

SOME OF THE STANDARDS / AUTHORITIES INVOLVED

TAX AUTHORITIES. They all have rules as to what can be included for taxation.

GAAP. USA & UK (Different). Generally Accepted Accounting Principles.

IFRS. International standards shortly to be adopted? (2016 SEC target?)

SEC. USA. Securities and Exchanges Commission. Has rules.

FASB. USA Financial Accounting Standards Board.

GASB. USA Government Accounting Standards Board.

AICP. USA. American Institute of Certified Public Accountants.

SSAP. UK. Statements of Standard Accounting Practice.

Sarbanes Oxley (SOX). USA introduced after ENRON, mainly for Public Companies.

DEALING WITH PRIVATE EQUITY / VENTURE CAPITALIST FIRMS

The PE firms are in the business of buying and selling companies on a relatively short cycle and they expect a good return. They finance the initial business purchase price by borrowing as much money as the bank will allow against the business performance, "Asset or EBITDA multiple," then make up the rest of the money with their own equity. The more responsible firms will be prudent about how much they borrow from the bank in order to reduce the risk profile on the business. They then operate the business with strong cash management to pay down as much of the fixed bank debt as possible. When they EXIT, the intent is to achieve a significant multiple of their equity from the sales price of the business. So the rules.

Company value is the main focus, and this is usually on an EBITDA multiple.

Cash can be tight and may even inhibit busiest investment, so understand the rules.

Venture capitalists do not like adventures, it is a hard-nosed business.

They will have an exit strategy, understand what it is and where you fit in after they have left.

They will often bring other lenders in maybe specialist "MEZZANINE" finance providers.

They are usually supportive and do have the ability to inject cash quickly to support their investment. If this is emergency funding, it may result in the managerial equity being reduced.

They are normally more supportive of management than a traditional board. They know that the less cost on the business the higher the EBITDA the greater the company value. This is more in line with instinctive management behavior to reduce costs. A board can often be full of its own importance and their own remuneration.

They call most of the shots most of the time?

An interesting management lesson learned from the PE / VC industry is the way they view a portfolio. For example, if they have 10 investments usually 2 or 3 will give excellent returns, the majority will be average and a couple will be dogs. Success will often depend upon identifying the dogs early and killing them before they drain time and cash. A variation of the management point that it is always better to spend time going from good to great than to sort out lost causes.

MAKE SURE THAT YOU DO YOUR DUE DILIGENCE ON THE PE FIRM, THEY WILL CERTAINLY DO IT ON YOU.

PSYCHOLOGICAL POINTS TO PONDER

THE POWER OF SELF BELIEVE

I have been in many negotiations, mainly sales related, all over the world. As with all negotiations one of the key things to do before getting engaged is to establish your **WALK AWAY POSITION** and make sure that you stick to it. One of my faults is that I rush and can make silly mistakes on quite simple numbers (I know! That's why it's at the back of the book). There have been a few occasions where I have worked out the bottom line price and because I believed that was the walk away position negotiated hard and won a contract. When back at the office and checked the numbers, I realized that I had made a mistake and actually had quite significantly over calculated the position and would have accepted a price much lower if I had realized my mistake.

THE POINT

I had created a believe system, by error, that I then went out and performed to! The result was above what would probably be considered economically rational.

THE OPPORTUNITY

Sometimes the full disclosure of the **REAL WALK AWAY POSITION** to a negotiating team is not a good idea. The GM may want to create targets for the negotiators that they believe **HAVE TO BE ACHIEVED**

THE POWER OF INFORMATION

The presence of information can often result in an improvement without the GM having to do anything else. I have seen this situation countless times. Ask someone to send you a KPI every day, or even better have a highly visible scorecard at the point of action. The people close to the situation instinctively try to improve and usually do!

Another point on information. Sometimes it is asked for because the originator needs to know it and be aware.

APPENDICES

	CHECK LISTS	A2
6	NEGOTIATIONS	A3
8	PROFIT IMPROVEMENT	A3
9	MANAGING BUSINESS FAILURE	A3
10	ACQUISITIONS	A4
11	MANAGE A DISTRESSED BUSINESS	A4
14	REVIEW CUSTOMERS	A5
22	FATAL ERRORS. REASONS BUSINESS FAIL	A3
26	LOOK AFTER YOURSELF	A5
28	THINGS WE MAY DO FOR FREE	A5
31	INCREASE PRICES	A5
32	NOT ALWAYS ABOUT MONEY	A5

NOTE
Check lists are taken from the *A DAY WITH A CEO Handbook*.

SOME COMMON TERMS AND ABBREVIATIONS   A6 — A10

CHECK LISTS

A POWERFUL TOOL

Checklists can be used as aides to doing things like the following,
OR
You should also create your own action checklists
to monitor progress and activity.
I am such a huge fan of check lists that I actually put things on that I have already done to have the satisfaction of crossing them off!!

**CHECK LISTS INCLUDED
FROM *A DAY WITH A CEO HANDBOOK***

NEGOTIATIONS
PROFIT IMPROVEMENT
MANAGING BUSINESS FAILURE
ACQUISITIONS
MANAGE A DISTRESSED BUSINESS
REVIEW CUSTOMERS
FATAL ERRORS THAT CAUSE BUSINESSES FAILURE
SOLVE A PROBLEM
LOOK AFTER YOURSELF
THINGS WE MAY DO FOR FREE
INCREASE PRICES
NOT ALWAYS ABOUT MONEY

♦ 6
NEGOTIATIONS

Do not fall in love with deal
Have a plan
Start early
Define objectives
Understand process
Define walk away position... Stick to it
Team work approach
Research other side
Do not get stranded
Build on consensus
Understand where power is
Make sure deal closed

♦ 22
FATAL ERRORS THAT CAUSE BUSINESS FAILURE

Forget importance of profit
Not accept personal responsibility
Fail to develop people
Manage everyone the same way
Concentrate on problems not objectives
Not own personal development
Be a buddy not a boss
Fail to set standards
Recognize only top performers
Try to manipulate people
Try to control results not influence thinking

♦ 8
PROFIT IMPROVEMENT

Introduce measure... KPIs?
Identify largest variable costs
Monitor and record results
Allocate dedicated teams
Focus on waste
Good to better is better than Poor to bad
Use Pareto Analysis to identify targets
Ask about grants
Involve everyone special exercises

Offer rewards for savings
Review all pricing
Review customer give aways
Review obsolete balance sheet items
Dispose of redundant assets
Review all accruals pre payments
Look at people costs
Ask finance if received any unallocated cash
Taxation opportunities

♦ 9
MANAGE BUSINESS FAILURE

Face the facts
Realize not end of world
Cut your losses quickly
Try to pay off debts
Protect / support your people

Do not take troubles home
Learn from mistakes
Salvage the best people and ideas
Give yourself a rest
Start again with stronger foundation

A DAY WITH A CEO — FINANCE   COPYRIGHT BRIAN MOORE   A3

10

ACQUISITIONS

A Potentially Game Changing Event,
But Expensive and Time Consuming With a High Risk.
Chance of Success 50%

Do not fall in love with deal
Stay objective and detached
Check cultural match
Check out major assumptions early
Allocate dedicated resource
Focus on customers
Pay attention to due diligence
Focus on cash flows

Look for off balance sheet liabilities
Assume owner managers will leave
Have an integration plan
Obtain expert opinion if not sure
Have a day one plan
Carry out one year review... Be honest

11

MANAGING A DISTRESSED BUSINESS
Profit improvement ideas

Elevate all controls to top
Especially cash / CQ sign off
Put in place daily cash reports
Introduce KPIs for key areas
Talk to key people secure services
Talk to banks get support. Stay close
Talk to suppliers secure credit
Reassure customers
Stop recruitment
Drive all past dues / arrears
Bring orders forward
Reduce stock and WIP
Review / sell surplus materials
Review increase prices
Consider pay cuts

Review working arrangement shifts
Reduce / stop overtime
Introduce short time working
Stop / reduce travel & expenses
Re-deploy surplus manpower
Introduce good communication plan
Collect debtors / receivables
Delay payments / creditors
Talk to credit agencies reassure them
Look at sub contract work, in-house?
Review all outstanding purchase orders
Talk to owners / shareholders. More cash?
Mothball plant if not used
Review customer credit limits
Introduce short-term forecasts

♦ 14 REVIEW CUSTOMERS
Acknowledge all customers are not right
Segregate customers into groups
Example: strategic / good / others / x list
Increase prices to poor customers
    aggressively (x list)
Be prepared to lose customers
Put controls in to accept new customers
Do not leave entirely to sales team

♦ 26 LOOK AFTER YOURSELF
Introduce stress reducing activities
Stay physically fit
Watch diet
Reduce alcohol, caffeine
Keep knowledge up-to-date
Read and network
Stay sociable and have outside interests
Take a break, clear the head

♦ 28 THINGS WE MAY DO FOR FREE
Telephone support training
Travel to meetings
Quality reports /audits
Carriage
Return goods no charge. Even if no fault
Literature
Reworks / returns / restocking
Technical advice and training
Learn from the airlines!!!

Try and charge wherever possible
100% profit, 100% cash

♦ 31 INCREASE PRICES
Be selective. Customers / products
Introduce minimum quantity order
Introduce minimum price invoice
Charge for extras, freight packaging etc.
Use price points
Bundle
De-bundle
Target low volume items high price
Target low value customers increase prices
Try not to use price to sell. FABS / USPS
Refuse credit notes
Refuse returns
Increase for late payments
Review distribution channels. Lost margin?
Be personally involved
Use pricing specialists
Only use cost as an indicator
Keep engineers away
Small and often. Better than big events
Review history of jobs. Learn and change

♦ 32 NOT ALWAYS ABOUT MONEY
Some Other Priorities

Safety of team members
Integrity of company
Quality and integrity of products
Personal issues of team members
Team morale
Team members welfare
Community support
Charity local and team members
Have fun reward performance

COMMON TERMS AND ABBREVIATIONS

ENERGY	**Human energy very important**	CASH COW	Mediocre business, but throwing of CASH
The 5 S's	Improvement technique SORT, STRAIGHTEN, SHINE, STANDARDIZE, SUSTAIN	CEO	Chief Executive Officer
ACMA	Associate Cost and Management Accountant (UK)	CFO	Chief Financial Officer
AGENDA	Everyone has one. Find it	CHAPTER 11	Court protection from creditors for distressed business. USA
AIM	UK small market	CHECK LIST	Items that require to be done
ALPHA	Initial test site	CHOP	Asian signature block used on contracts. Or fired
APOLOGY	Quick, if required. Very effective	CLOSE	Final point in a sale or contract
BANK SYNDICATE	Group of bankers that own a DEBT	COO	Chief Operating Officer
BELL	To open and close the NYSE	COVENANTS	Ratios used by banks for DEBT management
BELL CURVE	Graphical representation of statistical population	CPA	Certified Public Accountant (USA)
BILL OF MATERIALS	List of parts for a project or cost schedule	CPA	Critical path analysis
BOARD	Company supervising body. No further comments	CULTURE	Vital to success
BP	Blood pressure. Check it	DCF	Discounted Cash Flow
BREAK EVEN	Time fixed and viable costs covered by profit	DELAWARE	Business friendly state
BUSINESS REPORT	A series of numbers joined up by words	DISCOUNT	SOMETHING TO AVOID GIVING, BUT TO SEEK OUT
CA	Chartered accountant (UK)	DOWNSIZING	Process to reduce company / costs structure
CARPE DIEM	Seize the day. Get on with it	DUE DILIGENCE	Formal review process of key data. Usually on an acquisition
CASH	Life force for the business	EFTA	European Free Trade Association

COMMON TERMS AND ABBREVIATIONS

DISASTER PLANNING	Have a plan for worst-case scenario	**FDA**	Federal Drug Administration (USA)
DO IT NOW	Just get on with it	**FOB**	Free on Board. Exporting term
DOG	Boston Matrix poor company	**FOOTSIE**	Slang for London Stock Exchange
DORMANT	Company not actively trading. Name on shelf!	**Fortune 500**	Top 500 companies on Exchange
DOT	Dot the I's, meaning check small print	**Full Monty**	Total works, all in
E Mails	Eternal record. Beware	**FUTURES**	Anticipated stock prices and trading on
EARNINGS	Another name for PROFIT	**FX**	Foreign Exchange
EBIT	Earnings Before Interest and Tax	**FYI**	For your information
EBITDA	Earnings Before Interest and Tax Depreciation	**GAAP**	Generally Accepted Accounting Practice (USA)
EGO	Gets in the way of so much!	**GM**	Gross Margin
ENDORPHINS	Brain cell high following exercise	**GM**	General Manager
EXPENSES	Check them	**GONE UNDER**	Failed business
EPS	Earnings per Share	**GREED**	Anticipate it. A lot about!
EQUITY	Shareholders interest in a business	**GUESTIMATE**	A guess made to look more like a formal estimate
ESCROW	Independent place to hold docs / cash where both parties agree conditions to release	**HANG SENG**	Hong Kong Stock Exchange
ETA	Estimated Time of Arrival	**HOOK**	Device to attract interest and get person involved
EXERCISE	Important to stay fit	**HUMOR**	Very effective use carefully, especially internationally
FD	Finance Director	**I P O**	Initial Public Offering. Join an Exchange

COMMON TERMS AND ABBREVIATIONS

IAD	Internal Audit Director	LISTING	Join a stock exchange
INCENTIVE	Payment to get things done. Make sure targeted effectively	ROAD SHOW	Intensive meetings to raise finance
IQ	Can be missing in high places	LOW HANGING FRUIT	Easily identified opportunities
IR	Inland Revenue (UK)	LSE	London Stock Exchange. London School of Economics
IRR	Internal Rate of Return	M & A	Mergers and Acquisitions
IRS	Internal Revenue Service (USA)	M R P	Materials Requirement Planning
IT	Information Technology	MA AND PA SHOP	Small family business
J I T	Just In Time	MACHIAVELLIAN	Description of devious doing. Usually incorrect by someone that has not read "The Prince"
J T L	Just Too Late	MAX OUT	Best case scenario, top result
JET LAG	Can affect judgment	MBO	Management Buy Out
K P I	Key Performance Indicator	MBO	Management By Objectives
KAIZEN	Japanese word. Continuous improvement	MBWA	Managing By Walking About
KISS	Keep It Simple Stupid (Sugar)	MD	Managing Director
LEAN	Technique to improve processes	MEETINGS	Keep them short, effective and focused
LET GO	Sometime you just have to	MERGER	Do not exist. All acquisitions
LEVERAGE	Using one situation to improve another OR relationship of DEBT on the balance sheet	MEZZANINE	Add on debt / Financing
		MIND MAP / BRAIN PATH	Technique for creative thinking. Very effective

A8   COPYRIGHT BRIAN MOORE   A DAY WITH A CEO — FINANCE

COMMON TERMS AND ABBREVIATIONS

MISSION CREEP	Project drifting outside original plans. Controls required, if important	**PR**	Public Relations
NASDAQ	USA stock market	**QUICK RATIO**	Liquidity check. Current assets / current liabilities
NETWORKING	Meeting and talking to lots of different people in different scenarios. A learning experience usually	**RESUME / CV**	Creative writing opportunity
NYSE	New York Stock Exchange	**RISK / REWARD**	Calculate frequently. Key to capitalism
OEM	Original Equipment Manufacturer	**ROS**	Return on Sales
OUTSOURCE	Move production / services to outside provider	**SPC**	Statistical Process Control
PARETO	80% of value in 20% items (Approx.)	**SWOT**	Strengths. Weaknesses. Opportunities. Threats. Usually a complete waste of time, but it stimulates debate
PAY BACK	Return on investment. Need to calculate when and how	**SCAR TISSUE**	To describe some bad experiences. Negative learning experiences. Good for you? Sometimes!
PE FIRM	Private equity	**SEC**	Securities and Exchanges Commission (USA)
PERCENTAGE	Try to avoid using percentages when dealing in large numbers try and use actual cash amount	**SEED CAPITAL**	Starter cash for a new business
PI	Perpetual Inventory counting	**SEND**	Think twice before pressing!
POS	Point of Sale		

A DAY WITH A CEO — FINANCE   COPYRIGHT BRIAN MOORE   A9

COMMON TERMS AND ABBREVIATIONS

SENIOR DEBT	Top ranking debt	**TELEPATHY**	Does not really exist, but you probably rely on it!
SERENDIPITY	Unexpected good outcome from an unrelated event	**TEMPUS FUGIT**	Time flees, or flies. It really does. Do something special, make a contribution
SILENCE	Under-rated negotiating tool	**THANK YOU**	Little used expression
SLEEP	Important. Get some	**TIME MANAGEMENT**	Does not exist. It's YOU Management
SMALL PRINT	Check it if contract important	**TIME OUT**	Smell the daisies once in awhile
SOPORIFIC	My favorite word. Just never get to use it	**TRAINING**	Essential to keep everyone up to speed and effective
SPEED BUMP	Slang for a problem along the way	**TRUST**	Very important and it starts at the TOP
SPOT RATE	Currency exchange rate for the day	**TURN ROUND**	Process of improving a poor or failing business
STANDARD DEVIATION	Statistical population + /- 3 standard deviations	**UP SELL**	Add value to a sale with other services
STAR	Boston Matrix high performing company	**VACATION**	Take one
SUPPLIER	Very important, usually respect their profit. It may come back to haunt you	**VC**	Venture Capitalist
SWITCH SELL	Talk customer into another product than first interested in	**WEIGHT**	Watch it. You will feel better for it
SYNERGY	2 + 2 = 4 PLUS ?	**WHITE KNIGHT**	High net worth individual investing in a business
TALK	If you have to. Listening is far more effective	**WHY**	Ask it often!
TANKED	Bad situation, poor results. Missed forecasts	**WINDY**	Full of BS. Which is where Chicago obtained its name and not because of the weather
TEAM	Very important support structure	**WORK**	Something you are PAID to do. Keep the PAID to DO bit in mind!
TEASER	Brief document to attract interest. Often for an acquisition	**YIELD**	Return on assets or equities
YOU	Most important asset, look after it!	**R I P**	Run out of CASH

COPYRIGHT BRIAN MOORE — A DAY WITH A CEO — FINANCE

Made in the USA
Charleston, SC
02 June 2013